Becoming Transformational LEADERS In The Post-Biden Era

Leveraging Visioning, Veracity and Vocalization

Ervin (Earl) Cobb

Copyright © 2025 by Ervin Cobb

Published by RICHER Press
An Imprint of Richer Life, LLC

5710 Ogeechee Road, Suite 200-175, Savannah, Georgia 31405
www.richerlifellc.com

Cover Design: RICHER Media USA

Volume book discounts are available for groups, companies and organizations. Contact the publisher for information and order instructions.

No part of this publication may be reproduced, stored in a retrieval system, or transmitted in any form or by any means, electronic, mechanical, photocopying, recording, scanning, or otherwise, except as permitted under Section 107 or 108 of the 1976 United States Copyright Act, without prior written permission of the publisher.

Becoming Transformational Leaders In The Post-Biden Era
Leveraging Visioning, Veracity and Vocalization

Ervin (Earl) Cobb

1. Leadership 2. Leadership Development 3. Self-Help
[pbk : alk. Paper]

Paperback : ISBN-13: 979-8-9928996-0-3
Hardcover: ISBN-13: 979-8-9928996-1-0

PRINTED IN THE UNITED STATES OF AMERICA

June 2025

╬**RICHER Press**
An Imprint of Richer Life, LLC

RICHER Press is a full service, specialty Trade publisher whose sole goal is to *shape thoughts and change lives for the better.* All of the books, eBooks and digital media we publish, distribute and market embrace our commitment to help maximize opportunities for personal growth and professional achievement.

To learn more visit
www.richerlifellc.com.

Other Books By Ervin (Earl) Cobb

The Conscious Citizen
The Tough Questions The Average American Should Be Asking

Living a More Thoughtful Life
Thinkable Thoughts and Relevant Reflections

Why Is It So Hard
Becoming a People Person in the Post COVID-19 Era

Situations and Leadership
Short Stories and Lifelong Lessons

Leadership Front and Center
A Decade of Thought and Tutelage

The SMART LEADER and the Skinny Principles
How to Win and Lead within Any Organization

Driving Ultimate Project Performance
Transforming from Project Manager to Project Leader

The Official Leadership Checklist and Diary for Project Management Professionals

The Leadership Advantage
Do More. Lead More. Earn More.

God's Goodness & Our Mindfulness
Responding versus Reacting to Life Changing Circumstances

Focused Leadership
What You Can Do Today To Become a More Effective Leader

Pillow Talk Consciousness
Intimate Reflections on America's 100 Most Interesting Thoughts and Suspicions

Navigating the Life Enrichment Model™

Living a Richer Life
Getting the Most out of Life's Gifts and Circumstance

CONTENTS

CONTENTS

PROLOGUE

"A functioning, robust democracy requires a healthy educated, participatory followership, and an educated, morally grounded leadership." – Chinua Achebe

TRANSFORMATIONAL LEADERSHIP is a process whereby leaders engage with, and confidently influence others, to contribute to a common goal.

They do this by paying attention to their individual and collective desires, raising their interest and motivation, clarifying their expectations, and providing an ethical as well as social framework for critical thinking & decision making.

In so doing, *transformational leaders* can create positive and constructive change within people, within organizations, and within societies.

As researchers, scholars, and writers, we tend to think of *transformational leadership* mostly in corporate and business terms.

However, over my 35-year corporate career, and a dozen years of leadership development coaching after, I have grown to passionately endorse the need for more "*transformative leaders*" in all *levels* of private and public organizations.

My passion and concern has come from my somewhat clinical observations and analysis of the ever-changing, increasingly complex, and technologically driven world that we find ourselves in at this stage of the 21st century --- a world that is in need of *unselfish*, *intelligent*, *honest*, *humane*, *responsible* and *global* leadership; to seek near and long-term solutions versus continued nation-to-nation, region-to-region, and global conflicts.

Of course, this would require such leaders willing to focus on the needs of global humanity, realizable compromise and respect of "guard rails" to protect treaties and agreements from generation to generation.

As I briefly discuss in the *Introduction* of this book, the *"results"* of the 2024 Presidential Election in the United States, along with the condoning of vastly unusual Presidential appointments, and dozens of dismantling executive orders by the controlling Federal "leadership," has provided early insight into the apparent *malleability* of a key "guard rail" of America's democratic system of governance today, which is, the constitutional *"separation of powers."*

To be bravely honest, America's current fight to preserve democracy, as we know it, could be viewed as, and I quote, a *"tyranny of the majority."* This is a phrase used by the founding fathers *James Madison* and *Alexander Hamilton* in Federalist 51. It is something they feared was surely possible, especially if the leadership of all three of the branches of government teamed up to push for a more ideologically attractive, personally rewarding, and authoritarian form of government; this is instead of the *"balance of powers,"* which is critical to continuing the 237-year-old fight for the *aspirations* of *"we the people"* and a true *Democracy* as set forth in the U.S. Constitution.

My research and the analysis of many historians reveal that one of the major factors in the emergence of the significant increase in *"anti-federal government"* sentiment in the U.S., over the past decade, is anchored in the targeted use of communications techniques and styles associated with the classical, *Transformational Leadership* process.

According to the Institute of Policy Studies, *"The Republican campaign in 2024 relied on anti-government rhetoric, conspiracy theories, and violent innuendo (against FEMA, against the border patrol, and against Republican politicians that didn't toe the MAGA line) in order to do two things. These [transformational] strategies drew the disaffected to the polls, and they pushed others not to vote: to give up on politics altogether."*

It appears that it is such "messaging," masterfully commissioned by the leaders of one of America's two political parties, over decades since 1980, that fully began reaping the "desired rewards," beginning on *January 20, 2025.*

It is this *post-January 20, 2025,* period in American history, that I have coined, the *Post-Biden Era,* in the title of this book. To me, this is an obvious *"transition point,"* based on the diverging ideologies among the U.S. population; representing a possible and significant *pivot* in *governance* and *societal norms* going forward; a pivot that only American history will reveal.

In *Part Two* of this book, I share what I call the ten, *Key Leadership Relationships,"* as it relates to maximizing the leadership advantages associated with the Transformational Leadership process. You will notice that I intentionally weave into these concise discussions, some real-world *"How to use it"* guidance to help you consistently and successfully employ this set of attributes. These are *human traits* still strategically being used by the most successful Transformational Leaders around the globe.

In the *Epilogue* I examine the reasons why *Transformational Leadership* is most successful in leading those who feel either *disenfranchised* or *privileged.* In this dissertation, I offer a precaution and stress the need for *all of us* to *pay more attention and* realize that *"transformative powers"* can *"swing the pendulum"* in either direction.

From my research, experience and professional perspective, *"What you should embrace during your ascension to becoming a masterful Transformational Leader in the Post-Biden Era,"* is the embellishment of the following *actions* referenced in the book's subtitle, and discussed further in *Chapter One.*

> *"Leveraging Vision"* suggests a leadership style which embraces a clear visualization of the "what, how, when and the why."

> *"Leveraging Veracity"* suggests a leadership style which includes the singular truth, brazen authenticity, and undisputable acceptability.

"Leveraging Vocalization" suggests a leadership style which includes a voice which resonates broadly, coupled with influential communication skills, and an utterance of sincerity.

In the words of Kenneth Noland, a renowned American painter, who was thought of as an abstract expressionist, *"For me, context is the key - from that comes the understanding of everything."*

INTRODUCTION

"Leadership is not about the next election;
it's about the next generation." – Simon Sinek

LET ME BE CLEAR. Yes. Part Two of this book is a primer on leadership development and the relationships an effective transformational leader must have with ten key leadership attributes.

However, Part One of this book is less about leadership and more about the concept of more Americans *becoming* effective, transformational leaders. It's goal is to clarify and justify why using transformational leadership skills at this time in American history is needed to help defend our democracy from a long-time coming, ultra transparent, well-funded, and politically driven part of our citizenry.

Whether it's in a corporate board room, a local business, a national or local non-profit organization, a small church or large cathedral, a fraternity or a sorority, or a home-based group of concerned citizens, this nation, your state, your neighborhood, and your family all need transformational leaders as we move further into the 21st century.

Let me explain why, and why I wrote this book.

As you will find in Chapter One of this book, I discuss the fact that *leadership* is one of the most studied, most written about, and most trained disciplines in the history of mankind. I believe that it is not only because leadership, in its many forms, is omnipresent, and everywhere there is an exchange between humans, but also because of the "transformative results" that can occur through the effective use of the *transformative leadership style.*

What are some of these *"transformative results,"* you might ask?

Well, for millennia:

- Transformative results have fueled the development and growth of civilizations, as we know it, from small groups of indigenous peoples, to thriving metropolitans with billions of global citizens, and digital communications systems, which now links the East, West, North and South.
- Transformative results have enhanced man's transportation options, from the use of wheelless carts to horse drawn wagons, to bullet trains, to electric-powered automobiles, to supersonic airplanes to space travel; and
- Transformative results have changed human life from prehistoric existence as *Neanderthals* to *intellectual* beings whose cognitive and psychological development have avoided recent world wars, fed the hungry around the world, eliminated crippling diseases, and unraveled the effects of global climate change.

From the most complex to the simplest type of change in "human being" to a change in "human doing" is the need for someone to determine *"how to get from here to there."* And since leadership is not just "thinking about it," but actually "doing something about it," one must step-up, and show the way, by accepting and maturing in the role of a *transformative leader.*

Now, why did I write this book at this time?

To be honest, I must share that I have become obsessed. But not from an irresistible urge based on a conspirative or spiritual longing. This obsession stems from a passionate desire to constructively contribute to an effort to help fulfill the need for more *transformational leadership* within the American population, at this time in our country's history.

The passion driving this obsession comes from my experience as a 72-year-old, having grown up in the U.S. during the Jim Crow Era, and spending over 50 years, educating myself, taking advantage of opportunities to succeed, both intellectually and financially, beyond all expectations, and now to witness the return of a 1950's resurgence. The resurgence of a mentality and politics, regarding majority and male privilege; and an overt denial of the huge contribution of racial and cultural diversity to American life, as we know it today.

From the first time a sitting President refused to accept the results of a democratically and fairly held election, to a globally televised insurrection at the United States capital, to the rise of bizarre conspiracy theories, to the publicly acceptance of derogatory language by elected leaders, and to the reversal of a fifty-year-old constitutional right for women, this resurgence is slowly *transforming* American life.

A transformation of a marginally united and progressive America into one which has a genuine fear of one's neighbors, and one where its citizens must now choose sides in a politically manufactured, *"dive to the bottom,"* of human civility.

In the Prologue of this book, I share details of some glaring insights regarding some of the events and groups that were and still are strategically a part of this resurgence. In summary, my research indicates that the emergence of the significant increase in *"anti-federal government"* sentiment in the United States, over the past decade, is anchored in the targeted use of communications techniques and styles associated with the classical, *Transformational Leadership* process.

The facts are clear. This type of anti-federal government "messaging" by influential, ultra-conservatives, masterfully crafted and commissioned by the leaders of one of America's two political parties, is at the core, of this astonishing resurgence. And only American history, will record, it's true, impact.

All we know today, is that this is a resurgence, driven by an unsuspecting, broad, disenchanted, and bewildered coalition of American voters, which fully began reaping the "desired rewards," beginning *January 20, 2025,* with the inauguration of Donald Trump as the 47th President of the United States.

It is this *post-January 20, 2025,* period in American history, that I have coined, the "*post-Biden Era,*" in the title of this book.

I must admit that it was initially mind-boggling and overwhelming for me to process this resurgence and the presence of a selfish, hateful, and somewhat devilish spirit, beginning to linger, all across the United States of America.

However, once I spent some time thinking about what I was witnessing, which included a period where I researched and published a couple of books about possible causes, my thoughts moved from those of being overwhelmed to becoming gravely concerned.

It is my hope that, in this context, you will take the time needed to fully digest the dissertation and challenges set forth in Part One of this book and determine whether joining a new and more humanely centered army of transformational leaders is for you.

And, if so, then thoughtfully utilize the fundamental and action-oriented insights on how to deploy the *ten traits* associated with the most effective leaders discussed in Part Two in your personal and professional life.

This will not only kick-start your preparation to *become the transformational leader* that your organization, community, and nation needs at this time but start your journey to helping to preserve our system of democracy for generations to come.

PART ONE

CULTURAL WARS, POLITICAL STRUGGLES, AND LEADERSHIP

"Politics is an artifact of culture. It's a reflection: culture underwrites our politics." - James Davison Hunter

IT WAS OVER THIRTY YEARS AGO when sociologist James Davison Hunter coined the phrase "culture wars." Of course, the phrase "culture war" is a familiar metaphor for a political struggle caused by conflict between sets of social beliefs and cultural values.

Such political struggle is not a stranger to America's long history of internal political battles. From slavery, states' rights, and the fights over the size and control of the Federal government, to a long list of social and cultural issues, like abortion, sexuality, family values, and race, American politics has purposefully and prominently featured cultural preferences, beliefs, and differences as partisan rifts.

A host of controversial judicial, legislative, and partisan actions along with decades of political party messaging has led to the recent "pivot" away from traditional democratic governance, policy and practices. An astonishing pivot which is causing me and hundreds of millions of other Americans grave concern as I struggle to complete the manuscript of this book.

However, this book is not about personal struggle. It's about how *Transformational Leaders* must now *lead* during the post-Biden Era of the 21st century.

This is an Era in American history that is easily defined by the timely and calculated *results* of the unprecedented use of partisan political power. Power that was accumulated over decades by a heavily funded, intellectually coordinated, and elitist circle of one of America's two major political parties.

In the deceptively planned rush to cease the political power bestowed in him by only 49.8% of American voters in the 2024 Presidential election, Donald Trump, during his first 30 days in office, issued 76 executive orders enacting into law many of the conservative, partisan preferences developed by a conservative Think Tank, as documented in a publication titled, *"Project 2025."*

Note: You can review the description of all 76 Executive Orders as recorded in the U.S. Federal Register in the Appendix at the end of this book.

Then, came the Executive Branch's public disdain of the existing laws and new rulings of the U.S. Judicial Branch.

This was swiftly followed by the complicit acceptance of many obviously unlawful actions of the Executive Branch by the elected Republican officials controlling both houses of the United States Congress, which constitutionally has, and has historically used, the *power of checks and balances.* This "power" is a cornerstone of the U.S. Constitution and included by the founders as a barrier to constrain Executive Branch *power grabs* and intended to be used by the elected Representatives of *"We the People."*

Undeniably, this is truly an exceptional and unseen period in American society. Its substantial and overt threat to our country's Democratic form of government will only be factually interpreted by American history.

But, whether history interprets the *result* as an *"opportunistic political Coup,"* a *"tyranny of the majority"* as warned by America's founding fathers James Madison and Alexander Hamilton in Federalist 51, or *"just a major glitch"* in our country's experiment in American-style Democracy, there is no doubt that the basic fundamentals, associated with how *Transformational Leaders* can still effectively *lead* during the period, must significantly change.

If you are reading this book and consider yourself to be a *Transformational Leader* or someone aspiring to take on the mantle of such a leader, at this point in the 21st century, you may be asking yourself:

1. Why does this "pivot" in traditional democratic governance and heightened cultural wars necessitate a significant change in *Transformational Leadership?*

2. How will the roles of *Transformational Leaders* in America change?

3. How can *Transformational Leaders* leverage the new cultural and political order to the *country's* advantage?

Well. Part One of this book uses a systematic and factual-based approach to provide readily understandable answers to all three of these questions. It also points to this book's Appendix to provide further insight and concise records that might bear historical significance.

As you are about to intellectually engage and ponder the dissertation presented in Chapter One, you should keep in mind what it means to be or become a truly, *Transformational Leader.*

Being recognized as an effective *Transformational Leader* is about your skills and ability to create substantial change in individuals and organizations. Your primary role is to *motivate* and *inspire* others to achieve extraordinary personal and organizational success by transforming existing expectations, aspirations, perceptions, and values into something significantly substantial and better.

The *Transformational leadership* style is unique because it involves being conscious of and empathetic to unique experiences, circumstances, and individual journeys. Significant changes in social and political order can lead to a variety of outcomes, including changes in policies, social norms, political participation, and even societal structures. All impacting how individuals and organizations are *motivated* and *inspired.*

"If your actions inspire others to dream more, learn more, do more and become more, you are a leader."

— John Quincy Adams
Sixth president of the United States

CHAPTER ONE

CULTURAL WARS AND THE PRIMARY CHALLENGES TO TRANSFORMATIONAL LEADERSHIP

Why does this "pivot" in traditional democratic governance and heightened cultural wars necessitate a significant change in Transformational Leadership?

Cultural Wars and Transformational Leadership

BELIEVE IT OR NOT, the term "cultural war" is as old as mankind. Yet, there are many who may question the existence of culture wars altogether. But academics do define *culture wars* as a political struggle within all societies, caused by a natural conflict between sets of *social beliefs* and *cultural values.*

But the bottom-line reality and the most troublesome fact is that for centuries the term *culture war* has described a tireless fight of *beliefs,* which allowed clear and unquestionable *facts* and *logic* to take second priority to *personal ideals.*

Even though *culture wars* are not physical battles, they are ideological battles that have proved to have vast implications for societies and individuals.

These deeply emotional, mind-altering, and sometimes bitter battles have divided and polarized our country and its politics since America's founding. Their major effects on society as a whole is tribalism and sectarianism.

Sure. As human beings, we are tribal creatures by nature. But, when tribalism enters our state and national political systems to the extent they have in the late twentieth and Twenty-first centuries, society-wide turbulence arises from the political parties aggressive, selfish, and sometimes assiduous methods of encouraging extreme partisanship among their supporters.

According to a recent Pew Research Center survey:

"The overall share of Americans who express consistently conservative or consistently liberal opinions has doubled over the past two decades from 10% to 21%. And ideological thinking is now much more closely aligned with partisanship than in the past. As a result, ideological overlap between the two parties has diminished: Today, 92% of Republicans are to the right of the median Democrat, and 94% of Democrats are to the left of the median Republican."

Partisan animosity has increased substantially over the same period. In each party, the share with a highly negative view of the opposing party has more than doubled since 1994. Most of these intense partisans believe the opposing party's policies, and I quote. *"are so misguided that they threaten the nation's well-being."*

With America's culture wars having deep historical roots, dating at least as far back as the Civil War, and the extreme political, geographical, cultural and identity-based polarization throughout American society today, it is not a surprise to see, what were once purely ideological battles, are now, elitist battles for partisan political power, autocratic control of the Federal government, and its spending and legal authority.

According to Christopher Sebastian Parker, a professor of political science at the University of Washington, *"At the core of this fight is the threat to majority power and control."*

Parker argues further that, *"Status Threat — the theory that majority groups in a position of power feel like the gains toward equality for a minority group are losses for the majority — has contributed to the current backlash."*

It's not hard to justify Parker's argument and its merit, when he points to the *"take back our country"* and *"make America great again"* catchphrases of the most conservative fractions of the Republican Party.

Many Americans were overly concerned when Donald Trump famously announced his intention in 2023 to be a dictator *"on day one"* of his second term in office. Then, despite the ex-President's, *"me as a dictator"* statement seeming to be a real threat to America's democratic system of governance, a majority of American voters were not repelled by it. During the November 2024 Presidential election, 77,284,118 of them, or 49.8% of all votes casted, elected him as the 47th President of the United States.

Based on the obviously revengeful composition of President Trump's unprecedented number of executive orders in the first 30-days of his second term; the rapid, indiscriminate and across the board reductions in the U.S. Federal government workforce; and the Republican controlled Senate submissively approving Trump's vastly unqualified, inexperienced and perilous Cabinet appointments, it appears that our country will be *leaning more autocratic* versus *democratic* for a significant period of time.

Nevertheless, I believe a quote by Isaac Marion offers wise counsel for America, and for Americans, as it is *we the people,* who must stand up and address the current political and social dilemma. Marion said, *"We are where we are, however, we got here. What matters is where we go next."*

Hence, regardless of where we actually are today, whether in a *constitutional crisis* or a *coup d'état,* I believe that the answers to the *first question* I posed during the introduction of this Chapter can help all of us grasp the gravity of the *primary challenges* facing *Transformational Leaders* in this country as they re-tool to become more effective in filling some critical leadership gaps during this unprecedented period in American history.

Primary Challenges to Transformational Leadership

NOW, HERE ARE SOME of the primary challenges to *Transformative Leadership* that the answer to the question above exposes and reminds us to ponder at this time in American history.

As I touched upon in the introduction of this Chapter, the *Transformational leadership* style is unique because it involves being responsive and empathetic to unique *experiences*, *circumstances*, and individual *journeys*.

It's not difficult to imagine that the changes in social and political order being established in the first quarter of Donald Trump's second administration, and the significant "pivot" from historical norms, will lead to significant and rapid changes in *experiences*, *circumstances*, and individual *journeys* of hundreds of millions of Americans.

This will include changes in local, state and federal policies, social norms, political participation, and even societal structures. All of which will impact how individuals, employees, communities, and organizations are *motivated* and *inspired*.

It will also affect *social trust*, create *fear* of the unknown, and shatter historical *comforts* associated with *leading others* and *being led*.

I believe that the ongoing "pivot" away from traditional democratic governance and heightened cultural wars will require a significant change in the approach and fundamentals of how *Transformational Leaders* create substantial change within teams and organizations.

Based on my research and the work of many contemporary social scholars, the primary challenges will manifest themselves in six key areas. They are:

- Increased Polarization and Division within the American Society.
- Increased Level of Political Polarization.
- New Challenges in Communication and Dialogue.
- Further Erosion of Trust in Institutions.
- Growth of Extremism and Discontent; and
- Increased Focus on Identity Politics

Let's briefly discuss each of the primary challenges in these areas.

¤ Increased Polarization and Division within the American Society

The proclaimed victory by the conservative contingent of America's *cultural wars* and the devastating sense of lost by the liberal contingent will intensify existing divisions within the country.

This will make it harder for leaders, in general, to find common ground and build consensus among employees, team members and organizational units.

For *Transformational Leaders*, the challenges become even greater. This is due to the proven fact that with the aim of moving individuals, teams and organizations down the road of substantial change and improvement, leaders must be able to create a *long-term and common vision,* and gain a high level of *mutual trust* — two of the things that autocratic governance replaces with the compulsory control of *uncertainty* and the demand for *unwavering loyalty* of a society's populace anchored in fear.

¤ Increased Level of Political Polarization

An autocratic system of governance propelled by "woke" and generational-long cultural issues, can become highly and unimaginably politicized, leading to increased polarization and making it even harder for leaders to address complex problems in a constructive way.

When you factor in a globally consensus list of major issues the world governments are currently facing, including climate change, economic instability, threats of unfounded American tariffs on international commerce, food insecurity, the ongoing Fourth Industrial Revolution, and concerns about AI capabilities, cybersecurity, and geopolitical shifts, the increased complexity of the problems requires *transformational leadership* anchored in *less* and not *more* political polarization.

¤ New Challenges in Communication and Dialogue

The emotional intensity of current cultural conflicts in America can make it even more difficult for *Transformational Leaders* to engage in productive dialogue and find common ground among those holding opposing social, economic and political views. Of course, effective leaders must find common ground and agreement, to some extent, on the facts.

Now, speaking of facts, I am reminded of a timeless remark by John Adams, one of America's Founding Fathers, that gets at the heart of the dialogue and communications challenges facing all leaders today in this country, and I quote. *"Facts are stubborn things; and whatever may be our wishes, our inclinations, or the dictates of our passion, they cannot alter the state of facts and evidence."*

¤ Further Erosion of Trust in Institutions

When cultural conflicts become highly visible and divisive, it can erode trust in institutions, including government, education, and media.

Transformational leadership is characterized by inspiring vision, motivating followers, and fostering trust. This trust, in turn, leads to increased commitment, motivation, and positive outcomes for both individuals and organizations. Erosion in trust challenges the degree to which substantial changes and growth can occur.

According to the Pew Research Center in an October 2024 article:

"It's not exactly news that Americans are mistrustful of their federal government. What you may have heard less about is that trust in some historically respected institutions has also taken a hit in the post-pandemic years.

Trust in scientists has ticked down, as has the share of Americans saying that science has a positive impact on society. Trust in education is sagging. And recent years have found a record-low share of Americans with a positive view of the Supreme Court."

In most cases, these changes in opinion have a partisan cast, with supporters of one major political party shifting their views even as the other keeps faith. In this way, the long-standing narrative of institutional mistrust is increasingly intertwined with the extreme political polarization that has defined the current era.

¤ Growth of Extremism and Discontent

Social researchers and political scientists argue that if the end result of cultural wars is a *less democratic* and a *more autocratic* form of governance, a society is created where *extremism* and what may be viewed by the majority as *radical ideologies,* flourishing in veiled relationships, and hidden in discontent.

In recent years, researchers of several fields have developed theories and opinions to understand extremism and the radicalization process. One key factor that may promote an increased level of extremism and radical ideologies is an increase in *social exclusion.* In this context, social exclusion is defined as the state of being kept apart from others or the discounting of the contributions of minority groups to favor the majority. Indeed, experimental studies have provided initial evidence for a relationship between exclusion and extremism.

From a *Transformational Leadership* perspective, chances are, that within a highly social and culturally diverse country as the United States, substantially leading positive change becomes significantly more difficult if members of a team or an organization are naturally forced to focus more on individual and personal justice and inequity than on basking in the glory of group victory.

As once said by Barry Goldwater, *"Extremism in the defense of liberty is no vice. And moderation in the pursuit of justice is no virtue."*

¤ Increased Focus on Identity Politics

Intense cultural wars and extreme political polarization can lead to a focus on identity politics, which can overshadow other important issues, such as economic inequality and social justice. *The Wall Street Journal* columnist Gerald Seib recently noted, and I quote. *"Republicans were gearing up to focus 2022 midterm voters' attention on the "three I's" — inflation, immigration and identity politics."*

The following excerpt from a 2021 publication titled, *The Threat of Identity Politics* by Simon Heffer sums up this challenge.

"The emergence of identity politics proves many things; none of them edifying. It proves above all how no element of human misery or misfortune is above being exploited by political agitators for their own ends, and how people who have suffered unquestionable injustices — and the people of goodwill who sympathize with them — become the victims of confidence tricks by those who use identity politics to make progress with extreme political aims that would otherwise be hopeless to secure."

Effectively *leading* individuals, teams and organizations within this manner of social and political environment will require a special focus on inspiring and motivating others regardless of their personal *identity* and empowering, growth, innovation, and collaboration even within autocratic environments.

In summary, you can easily imagine even from just this *rudimentary level* of candid discussion on the topic, the level of impact this post-Biden Era "pivot" away from traditional democratic governance will have on the lives and futures of hundreds of millions of Americans who value the rights bestowed to them by the United States constitution, and view *community*, *social progress*, and *humanity,* differently.

It should not be difficult for the average American to now, understand the need for stronger, and more courageous, civic-minded, public and private sector leadership, to *counter* or *minimize* a generation of loss in social and economic progress in a country with a history of democratically, surviving social struggle.

I believe that this country's long and rich history, strongly suggests a *Transformational Leadership* focus and skillset, which is more aligned with shaping a new democratic-leaning future, supported by an unflappable plurality of Americans, and targeting the "real-world," twenty-first century challenges — a*nd* ***not****, just an attempt, to put the* ***genie****, that escaped on November 5th 2024, back in the bottle.*

"Coming together is a beginning; staying together is progress; working together is success."

— Henry Ford

American industrialist and business magnate

TRANSFORMATIONAL LEADERSHIP AND PLURALISM

"The great American tradition is one of pluralism, not exclusive secularism. The strength of our country is reflected in the contributions that we all make to the common good." — Donald Wuerl

THE LEADERSHIP CONCEPT and disciplines associated with what is defined as *Transformational Leadership* is celebrating its fifty-first birthday this year. The origins of transformational leadership in the United States can be traced back to 1973 when sociologist James V. Downton first introduced the phrase.

Over the past half century, the critical components associated with the concept of transformational leadership have practically remained the same. *Transformational Leaders* around the world have been recognized for their ability to intellectually *stimulate*, *motivate*, and *influence* others by embracing and enthusiastically employing *empathy* to empower and *transform* organizations; and produce beneficial effects.

However, over the past half century, the world as we know it has also "transformed" significantly. Among these transformations are political, economic, medical, psychological, technological, and social changes which have *affected* the "target" of this leadership concept, which is, of course, the diverse, human population.

Yet still, none of us can escape the fact that *we spend most of our lives either leading or being led.*

Another significant fact is that regardless of individual attempts to mentally suppress the disappointment or excitement of new laws and social changes driven by autocratic-leaning politics and governance, such changes decisively reduce the levels of pluralism and multiplicity within society that are vital to effectively leading transformational initiatives.

As a *Transformational Leader* in this post-Biden Era, you will most certainly face teams and organizations with individuals noticeably affected by these changes in the national and local political and social environment. It shouldn't be surprising to find unfavorable impacts on professional attitudes, and the lack of the ability for many individuals to be intellectually *stimulated*, *motivated*, and *influenced.*

According to Joel Rosenthal, the President of the Carnegie Council for Ethics in International Affairs, *"Pluralism is one of democracy's essential virtues. Diversity of thought, motivation, lifestyles, and more to coexist within a political body is indispensable to democracy."*

Below is a comparison of the differences between Democratic versus Autocratic motivations.

Autocratic Motivations	**Democratic Motivations**
Centralized Control	Values
Obedience & Conformity	Self-Motivation
Speed & Efficiency	Inclusivity
Hierarchy & Authority	Innovation & Creativity
Short-Term Gains	Empowerment

As you will note from this comparison, the differences in motivation, even when there is an agreement on the ultimate goals and objectives, autocratic-minded teammates and democratic-minded teammates may desire to take significantly different paths.

To lead individuals and teams with conflicting motivations influenced by partisan and autocratic preferences, *Transformational Leaders* must dig deep in their leadership "toolbox" and take advantage of the *Ten Absolute Attributes* discussed in Chapter Two. It is true, resolving conflicts of this nature is an *art* and not a *science.*

THE EXPANDED ROLES OF TRANSFORMATIONAL LEADERS IN AMERICA

How will the Roles of Transformational Leaders Change?

WITHOUT QUESTION, LEADERSHIP IS one of the most studied, documented, discussed, celebrated and sometimes mystifying subjects that mankind has encountered. An apparent confusion and transformation of leadership theories have been going on for centuries, as revealed in the philosophical writings from Plato's Republic.

From the most complex to the simplest type of change in "human being" to a change in "human doing" is the need for someone to determine *"how to get from here to there."* And since leadership is not just *"thinking about it,"* but actually *"doing something about it,"* one must step-up, and show the way, by accepting and maturing in the role of a *leader*.

During my review of contemporary literature on *leadership styles* over the past twenty-five years, I have become convinced that the evolution and expansion of leadership styles is merited.

My reasoning is simple. It is quite obvious that in order for a leadership style to be effective, it must be compatible with the organization, the company, the situation, the team, and the leader's strengths.

In *Focus Leadership: What You Can Do Today to Become a More Effective Leader*, the first and most reflective book on leadership development that I have published, I shared, *"I have learned through the school of hard knocks that effective leadership requires adaptability and a range of approaches to achieve goals."*

Below is a comparison of a short list of leadership *styles* that have been documented, practiced, and evaluated most recently. You will find an expanded list in the Appendix (Page 179).

COMPARISON OF LEADERSHIP STYLES

Transformational Leadership	The Leader creates substantial change for team members as well as organizations and motivates and inspires them to reach extraordinary success. Expectations, aspirations, perceptions, and values are transformed into something better.
Democratic Leadership	The Leader builds on empowering team members to participate in decision-making, with a strive toward consensus.
Visionary Leadership	The Leader focuses on the long-term results and builds on participation, communication, and goal setting.
Commanding Leadership	The Leader maintains tight control with high clarity in rules, roles, and expectations and makes all the decisions.
Servant Leadership	The Leader focuses on improving people, society, and organizations and serves others, which leads to strong ethics, and engaged, motivated employees.
Transactional Leadership	The Leader builds a clear structures of rewards and punishment for different levels of performance and focuses on results, efficiency, and performance rather than people and relationships.
Autocratic Leadership	The Leader holds all the decision power, rarely consults others, which leads to low engagement and sometimes create toxic environments. This style is useful in a crisis when control and fast decisions are crucial.

Of all of the documented leadership styles that have surfaced over the years, I have found that *transformational leadership* clearly stands out from all others. This unique leadership style is a challenging style to fully deploy. However, the style is the best choice when a situation demands the timely implementation of major performance and productivity improvements at the team or organizational levels, and when obvious barriers to success exist.

The Traditional Roles of Transformational Leaders

THE TRADITIONAL ROLE OF *Transformational Leadership* is to significantly enhance organizational innovation and to primarily focus on the most charismatic and affective elements of leadership.

However, the most effective *Transformational Leaders* have skills and personal strengths associated with four traditional roles. For discussion purposes, I commonly characterize the four *Traditional* Leadership roles as follows.

1. The Role of *The Stimulator*
2. The Role of *The Confidant*
3. The Role of *The Influencer*; and
4. The Role of *The Motivator*

As with all leadership styles, each role is defined by specific targets, focuses, and goals. Here is a brief overview the four *Traditional* roles of *Transformational Leadership*.

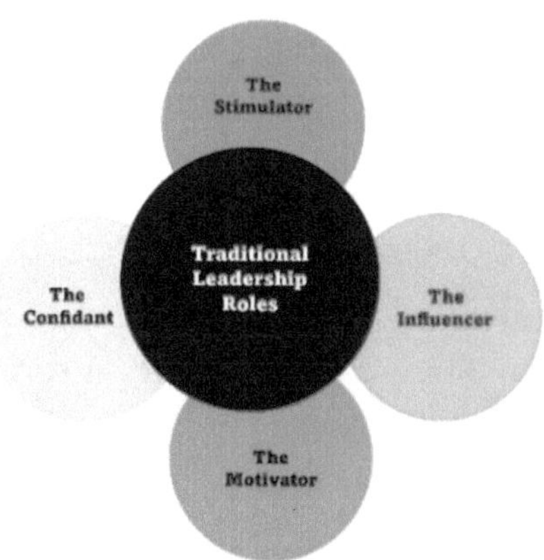

The Role of The Stimulator

The role of the *Stimulator* is to encourage the idea of thinking independently, creatively, and critically. The goal is to ultimately stimulate a significant level of individual, team and organizational innovation and problem-solving. The leader's primary focus in this role is on challenging assumptions, seeking diverse perspectives, fostering creativity, embracing innovation and encouraging critical thinking.

The Role of The Confidant

The role of the *Confidant* is to be attentive to the unique needs, aspirations, and concerns of each individual and team member. The goal is to be perceived as a mentor and coach helping individuals, teams and organizations reach the targeted objectives. The primary focus is on being supportive and empathetic of individual and team needs. In this role, the leader also creates supportive environments, recognizes individual and team contributions, and builds authentic relationships.

The Role of The Influencer

The Transformational Leader's role as the *Influencer* involves acting as a role model, inspiring individuals and teams by demonstrating high ethical standards and a commitment to the organization's values. In this role, the leader consistently acts with integrity, demonstrates a strong moral compass, builds trust and respect, and communicates a compelling vision.

The Role of The Motivator

In the role of the Motivator, *Transformational Leaders* inspire and motivate individuals, teams and organizations to achieve a shared vision. The goal is to foster a sense of purpose and to encourage the maximum performance of individuals teams and organizations.

By articulating a compelling vision, inspiring everyone to achieve it, and creating a sense of personal commitment and enthusiasm, the leader becomes a *master motivator* and a major factor in ensuring that all targets are achieved or surpassed.

As you can see, successfully executing all four *traditional roles* of *Transformational Leadership* can be a *tall order* and a *heavy lift* for even the most skilled and committed leader.

However, when a transformational leader must also execute such a feat within an environment filled with unprecedented political and cultural uncertainty, it becomes clear that the role of the traditional leader must be expanded to address the new challenges of the post-Biden Era in America.

The New "Interventional" Roles of Transformational Leaders in the Post-Biden Era

AS I SAT AT MY WRITER'S DESK in February 2025, I surprisingly struggled to complete the first draft of this manuscript. Then, I was moved to spent a few minutes reflecting on my reason for taking on this project. I repeatedly asked myself, *"Why do I feel so strongly about the need to write a book about becoming a Transformational Leader during this time in American history."*

Of course, when I began to gather my years-long research on the topic of becoming a *Transformational Leader* in December 2023, I could not even imagine, at that time, the level of *shock* and *awe* that would be caused by the initial Executive Orders issued during the first few months of the second Trump Administration. This is despite the clear warnings of possibly more political chaos if Donald Trump would win the 2024 Presidential election.

However, prior to writing the later sections of this book's manuscript, and recognizing the punitive nature of Donald Trump's initial Executive Orders, I created the time to impartially review what was happening.

When I noticed the controlling political party within the U.S. Congress not willing to perform their constitutional role of providing *checks* and *balance* of illegal Presidential power, and the Executive Branch's obvious goal to destroy more than 80-years of hard-fought, positive international and domestic achievements, I began to deeply ponder my 72-years as an American citizen.

Let me share with you a little of my relevant background as an American citizen. The most influential element in shaping my life in this country was being born in the 1950's and having to live through the Jim Crow Era in the United States.

Yet, in spite of the cruel Jim Crow Laws and the dehumanizing cultural challenges of segregation and constitutionally sanctioned racism, I somehow managed to not only survive but to actually thrive along the path of becoming a corporate professional.

In hindsight, it seems that the path that I navigated to become a corporate leader seems a little mystifying, based on my start in life. But, for sure, it was a path that was filled with unforeseen challenges and opportunities.

It's hard to believe the number of great *leadership development* opportunities that eventually came my way. They included *leading* technology development when I was a young computer engineer in the 1970s; *leading* major equipment manufacturing projects as a manager in the 1980s; *leading* large business teams within Fortune 100 companies as an executive in the 1990s; and *leading* a venture capital backed internet start-up, and surprisingly a couple of family-financed entrepreneurial business franchises in the early 2000s.

It was through these opportunities, and the good fortune of having a loving family, supportive friends, and strong mentors that helped me see and to stay on the path leading me to my current position in life.

I fondly recall the mentors who *"intervened"* and helped me climb some of the higher mountains along the way as I strived to achieve my career goals as a technologist, and eventually as a corporate leader.

In fact, it was the empathy, motivation, encouragement and *"intervention"* of my mentors in my career, and in my life, which contributed greatly to my efforts to *become a Transformational Leader*. And for me, as an American, to realize the benefits of the gradual, 237-year evolution of the U.S. Constitution, and the positive growth of America's democratic-style of governance over this time.

Having shared this portion of my personal history, it should not be surprising that while I was in the process of considering what *additional roles* would enhance the skillset of *transformational leaders* practicing in the United States during this new political and social era, I concluded the following:

> *"While navigating new cultural and political "spaces" within America's more autocratic style of Federal governance, Transformational Leaders should enhance their leadership skillset with new roles that support strategic "intervention" to increase the probability of achieving individual, team and organizational success."*

As a result, I have advantageously developed, and have introduced to the global leadership community four new *Transformational Leadership* roles. These new roles are intended to be combined with the four *Traditional* roles to help *Transformational Leaders* navigate the above-mentioned, cultural and political "spaces."

I have characterized each of these four *Interventional Leadership Roles* of *Transformational Leadership* as follows.

1. The Role of *The Navigator*
2. The Role of *The Humanizer*
3. The Role of *The Salvager*, and
4. The Role of *The Elevator*

Here is a brief overview of the four *Interventional Leadership Roles* of *Transformational Leadership.*

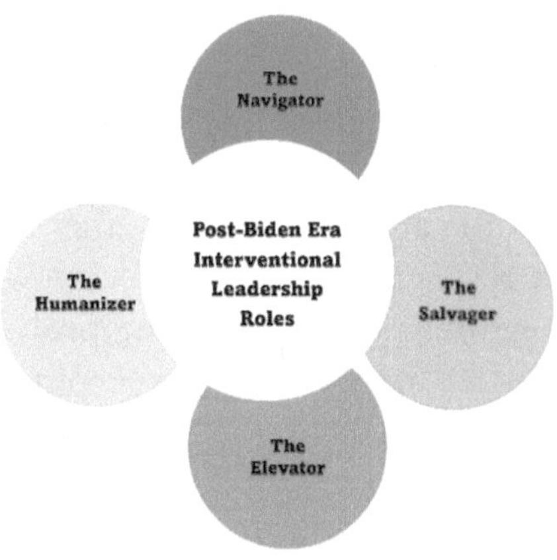

The Role of The Navigator

The role of the *Navigator* is to guide and assist individuals, teams or organizations through complex political and social "spaces" where traditional democratic approaches must be deployed to help navigate around new autocratic-leading protocols. The goal is to gain or retain bipartisan support and resources to maintain *Transformational* momentum.

The Role of The Humanizer

Similar to the function of humanizers in Artificial Intelligence, or AI, that are associated with bridging the gap between machine-generated text and human expectations, the role of the *Humanizer* in *Transformational Leadership* is to identify and to take the lead in making the necessary ***modifications*** in human communications required to "bridge" destructive "disconnects." These disconnects or failures in effective communications normally occur when ***more autocratic-leaning*** and ***traditionally democratic-lending*** "mindsets" collide.

The Role of The Salvager

The role of the Salvager is to intellectually engage and lead timely actions necessary to rescue, or retain critical transformational momentum. The goal is to prevent, during troublesome social or political moments, further danger, damage, or destruction of the individual, team or organizational progress that has been made toward achieving the ultimate *Transformational* goals.

The Role of The Elevator

The role of the *Elevator* is to convincingly articulate and carry messages, requests and needs from individuals and team members to higher levels of authority where the broader and deeper perspective of a respected leader will be viewed more favorably. The goal is to significantly increase the probability of success in achieving the desired outcome and the ultimate *Transformational* objectives.

The Expanded Roles of Transformational Leadership

Roles	Leadership Focus and Responsibilities
Stimulator	Innovation, Creativity, Goal Setting, Challenges
Confidant	Mentor, Empathic, Purpose, Strength & Skills
Influencer	Role Model, Walk-the-Walk, Enthusiasm, Values
Motivator	Vision, Optimism, Inclusion, Productivity
Navigator	Guidance, Assistance, Momentum Tracker
Humanizer	Bridge Maker, Communications Connector, Modifier
Salvager	Coach, Engager (social & political context), Rescuer
Elevator	Introspection, Message Carrier, Translator, Interpreter

In Summary

I BELIEVE THAT ALL EIGHT leadership roles will be necessary to allow *Transformational Leaders* to become more effective throughout transformational efforts while navigating challenging, cultural and political, "spaces."

In combination, the *Traditional* and *Interventional* leadership roles strengthen a leader's ability to *leverage* three of the most important things that *Transformational Leaders* can bring to any major transformation, which are: *Vision*, *Veracity* and *Vocalization.*

In the following section, I will discuss the strategic art of creating *leadership leverage,* and why *Leveraging Visioning, Veracity and Vocalization* or LV3 is a unique and powerful strategy designed to enhance a leader's chances for delivering *transformational success* as well as delivering, as a byproduct, broader *cultural change* within the host communities.

"For me the greatest beauty always lies in the greatest clarity."

–Gotthold Ephraim Lessing,
German writer, philosopher, dramatist, publicist and *art critic.*

CREATING LEADERSHIP LEVERAGE FOR TRANSFORMATIONAL SUCCESS: VISIONING, VERACITY AND VOCALIZATION

THE ART OF CREATING LEVERAGE

LEVERAGE IS ABOUT USING what you have to achieve more than you otherwise could, whether it's financial resources, relationships, time, or other assets. Leverage is an art that must be perfected. When skillfully deployed, it is a powerful tool for maximizing impact and achieving desired outcomes in various aspects of business, society and life.

In the discipline of *Transformational Leadership,* it's not as simple as just knowing how to leverage *resources*, *time*, and *assets*. The most effective leaders are well aware of the techniques of leverage and many are exceptionally well skilled at selecting the *best strategy* to generate the best outcome.

However, the most perplexing challenge has always been convincing a leader to similarly value the need to develop the unique leadership skills required to truly get the maximum leverage from project, team and organizational *relationships.*

The most successful and effective leaders understand that strategically placing themselves in the position to succeed is heavily dependent on the depth and the quality of their relationships with all key members of the team or organization.

The *right strategy* and a *deliberate focus* on *leveraging* relationships can also lead to encouraging broader societal changes. Such changes may include promoting civil dialogue among neighbors, respect for cultural differences as well as the rule of law, and strengthening public institutions that support the common good, especially during times of political and social upheaval. In the following sections I will outline how the *right strategy* and *deliberate focus* can best be deployed.

LEVERAGING TRANSFORMATIONAL SUCCESS TO GAIN BROADER CULTURAL CHANGE

IF YOU HAVE BEEN INVOLVED in any kind of major change or transformation activity in the past, you are aware that the most significant factor in creating significant and sustainable change is the acceptance of a *change in culture.*

As a *Transformational Leader,* accurately and consistently visioning and articulating challenges and opportunities connected with *culture change* must be a top priority. As once said by Marcus Buckingham, the English author, motivational speaker and business consultant:

> *"Culture is the everyday behaviors of your people. It's how they show up when no one is looking."*

The significant changes in *political*, *financial*, *ideological*, and *cultural* priorities, we all are witnessing today as the early post-Biden era in America unfolds, can naturally complicate a leader's perception of the *motivational*, *emotional* and *transformational* appetite for major changes for most of the working population.

However, from a historical and more comprehensive view of the current situation, I believe the complications and challenges associated with abrupt changes in *politics* and *culture* can also yield specific opportunities for leveraging transformational success, and for gaining broader cultural change. Since the basic fundamentals associated with *Transformational Leadership* can foster private and public innovation, and promote a shared vision of a positive future, it can also encourage all that are involved in the process to gain a broader perspective of the institutions and people who honestly serve the "common good."

It is this natural byproduct of *Transformational Leadership* that provides leaders opportunities, during disruptive and challenging political and social times, to successfully deliver on two important fronts.

The first is the opportunity to deliver successful improvement in productivity and industrial output for clients during difficult times of economic and social uncertainty.

The second is the opportunity to play a major role in leading the determined effort required throughout the country to deliver, as described by civil rights leader and Georgia Congressman John Lewis, *"the good trouble,"* needed to retain and protect America's fragile, democratic style of governance.

I strongly believe that *Transformational Leaders* can do this by strategically *leveraging* their advantageous and trusting *relationships* with others; by reminding them of the value and the necessity of making informed decisions; by pointing to possibly misguided and undereducated voting choices; by recapping the dire consequences associated with extreme partisanship and clinging on to myopic views of situations; and by professionally *conveying* the importance for all Americans to take voting and their constitutional and civic responsibilities more seriously.

All of a leader's discussions in these areas should be private and inconspicuous, but they should carefully lean into their respected relationship and their personal knowledge of each individual's circumstances, fears, and genuine concerns. The publicly known financial and social struggles being faced by millions of Americans during this obviously politically generated upheaval should be deliberately highlighted.

However, *conscientiously* shared in a fashion which will allow various *personalities* to grasp and examine the facts, unrealistic expectations, and the potential impacts of their own unconscious behavior, beliefs and actions without a perception of coercion.

Okay. I know that there is a need for me to provide a little more insight and contemporary context here.

First. Here are the two *"knowns"*, as of the writing of this book.

1. The unprecedented "pivot" away from America's over 200-years of democratic governance was certainly not a military coup or overnight event. It required an over 40-year effort by the Republican Party to maneuver and gain a super 6-3 majority in the U.S. Supreme Court.

   The regaining both the U.S. Senate and the U.S. House of Representatives in 2024 with historically small majorities was the result of extreme gerrymandering at the State level and a "win at all cost" mentality, draped in a disingenuous but consistent media focus on nationally divisive and ultra conservative issues; and

2. As mentioned at the beginning of this Chapter, it was the re-election of Donald Trump, a two-time convicted felon, and his mystical ability to win the November 2024 Presidential election that paved the way for an autocratic-leaning and revengeful Executive Branch.

   In hindsight, as I sit here at my writer's desk in April 2024, the vast majority of Americans are now aware, that the second Trump Administration is a valid threat to dismantle decades of highly professional, competent, bipartisan and world-class expertise within the Federal Government workforce and agencies; and in a position to take advantage of an opportunity to replace it with selfish cronyism and unwarranted presidential loyalty.

   Yet, the most educated Americans are sitting on the sidelines, not willing, or afraid, to call *"a duck a duck,"* and are well aware that the country is in a *"constitutional crisis"* where, for the first time in our country's history, politically and judicially, there are no good answers.

Now, here are the two *"encouraging signs"*, that I have observed, which may provide the opportunity for *Transformational Leaders* to deliver both success for their clients as well as help to minimize any long-term change caused by this unthinkable and disruptive tyranny that our country is currently experiencing.

1. Yes. Donald Trump's electoral victory in the November 2024 election was electorally substantial. However, it relied heavily on a tougher stand on *"unlawful"* immigration at the U.S. Southern border, and a mis-leading and broad perception that a good post-pandemic economy was much worse than reality when viewed globally.

   Conservative voices has convinced their supporters that the victory was an American voter "mandate," yet, Donald Trump only won the national popular vote with a plurality of 49.8% and currently has a falling approval rating.

   To me, this can be bi-partisanly viewed as an indication that America's first taste of authoritarian rule might propel a substantial swing toward democratic-leaning candidates versus undeserved party loyalty in the 2026 mid-term and the 2028 Presidential elections; and

2. Even with the dramatic political and social disruption in this early period of the post-Biden era, America's capitalist-minded financial and business communities will depend on significant improvements that *Transformational Leaders* can provide in maintaining economic growth and controlling consumer prices, even with the Trump Administration's unjustified and irrational global tariff war.

By delivering results, as described above, which can achieve much improved performance targets while building and leveraging deep and quality relationships, *Transformational Leaders* can also lead the development and growth of a civic-minded, and democratic-leaning, population of American voters.

These are voters capable of saving or salvaging what may be left of the American democracy we have known for over 237-years, and, maybe, preventing an extended period in American history similar to what followed the Compromise of 1877.

The Compromise of 1877 was a congressional and presidential "deal," which ended the *Reconstruction Era* in America, and led to government-sanctioned segregation, cruel Jim Crow Laws in the South, and the widespread disenfranchisement of Black voters for over eighty-years.

A FOCUSED STRATEGY FOR TRANSFORMATIONAL LEADERSHIP AND BROADER CULTURAL CHANGE

IT IS NO SECRET that within all leadership styles, it is encouraged that leaders should *leverage* their strongest and most admired attributes. This approach can lead toward maximizing their overall effectiveness. By understanding and leveraging their unique strengths, all leaders can make more informed decisions, enhance their influence, create positive change and more productive work environments.

However, as I discussed and outlined in the previous section, in addition to delivering significant and positive change for their clients, a natural byproduct of *Transformational Leadership*, is the unique opportunity during disruptive political and social times to successfully play a major role in leading the determined effort required to protect America's democratic style of governance.

To successfully seize this unique opportunity, my research and experience, has led me to believe that a *focused communications strategy* is critically important when leading major transformations within a populace where many middle to lower class constituents have become, what I call *"psychologically pickled,"* and are now highly reluctant to change; even when it is clearly in their best interest.

Here is a brief explanation of what I mean by *"pickled,"* and an argument for the significance associated with the understanding of this well-intended, allegorical characterization.

As you may recall, in the Prologue of this book, I mentioned that my research and the analysis of many historians reveal that one of the major factors in the emergence of the significant increase in *"anti-federal government"* sentiment in the United States over decades, *resulting* in America's recent "pivot" toward a more authoritarian style of governance, was anchored in a *focused communications strategy* deployed by ultra-conservatives and the Republican Party in a relentless fashion.

It is important to understand the effectiveness and the broader *results* gained with this strategy. If an effective *"counter"* to this decades-long communications strategy is to be deployed, it must be thoughtful, well-planned, and well-executed to specifically address the reality of the following:

> When the Republican and other ultra-conservative's heavily financed communications strategy, was ecstatically embraced and amplified repetitively by conservative talk radio and national news media for decades, it *transformed* and conditioned how their targeted constituents *minds* would forever *hear* and *digest* information on social, political and religious topics.
>
> The slogans, *"Fair and Equal," "Us versus Them," "Red versus Blue," "The Dems," "The Liberals," "Red Meat," "The Left and the Right,"* and *"The Deep State"* coupled with Federal and State Party unity and 21st century broadcast technology, simply *locked in,* and *rewarded* deep rooted, centuries old, intuitive thoughts and beliefs. Then came the "pickling" effect, turning what may have once been a sweet, tender cucumber, into what is now a crunchy pickle, incapable of returning to the original state of being.
>
> As being *"psychologically pickled,"* a huge number of American voters now only expect to hear short and clearly articulated messages, in consistent repetition, and embodying only a few and easy to remember points, which resonate with narrow-minded thoughts and long-held beliefs. The voices that deliver the messages are expected to be strong, persuasive, unwavering, and willing to fight for and validate their beliefs as being "right," regardless of the opinions of others, the facts,

or the truth; aka Fox News, Fox Business, Breitbart, Newsmax and OAN.

Leveraging Visioning, Veracity and Vocalization or LV3 is a unique communications strategy designed for *Transformational Leaders* to efficiently deploy to counter the successful strategy being relied on by today's Republican Party in their major role to legislatively sustain America's current "pivot" away from democratic governance. It is designed to be deployed seamlessly within the natural framework and daily activities of the *Transformational Leader.*

The LV3 strategy can transparently leverage the role of any *Transformational Leader.* It allows leaders to empathetically mentor, encourage, and develop permanent avenues for *self-initiated* critical and conscious thought. The goal is to lead individuals, teams and organizations to a less myopic and broader view of the *humanistic* value of *critical thinking* and the *common good.* Such a perspective can be easily targeted to f*ocus* on both the possible *success* of transformational projects, as well as the possible *improvements* in American social and political life.

As the "sparks" of millions of these types of professional and valued *relationships* ignite into flames of *understanding* and *bipartisanship* across the country, they could become the seeds needed to create the plurality of more thoughtful American voters required to grasp near-term civic opportunities to *"turn the ship around"* and recapture, and improve, the evolving democracy of earlier periods in American history. This effort will provide an additional weapon in the fight of protecting America's fragile democracy. However, it will take time, focus, and the unique skills of *Transformational Leaders* willing to engage in this battle. But, of course, as once said by Bill Gates, co-founder of the Microsoft Corporation, *"The most brilliant strategy won't lead to success unless it's executed effectively."*

As I have reviewed the LV3 strategy with leadership scholars, cohorts and political thought-leaders across the country, they all generally agreed with the concept of *Transformational Leaders* deploying the LV3 strategy in their transformation efforts during this time in America's history. They also agreed with the idea that leaders helping others gain a greater respect for *the common good* is quite plausible. Most thought-leaders regard the LV3 strategy's *strategic targeting*, and its *simplicity in execution*, as the primary success factors in "countering" the long-held Republican Party's *"pickling"* communications strategy. Leveraging existing *relationships* utilizing the three overarching leadership attributes of *vision*, *veracity* and *vocalization* is also a major factor.

Leveraging Vision embraces a clear visualization of the "what, how, when and the why. *Leveraging Veracity* illuminates a characteristic singular truth, brazen authenticity, and undisputable acceptability. *Leveraging Vocalization* conveys a confident voice which resonates broadly and a calming utterance of sincerity.

On the next page you will find a summation of the essence of the LV3 communications strategy along with a graphical interpretation of the environment it creates; followed by a portrayal of the eight roles of effective *Transformational Leaders*.

It is my hope that all *Transformational Leaders* get involved in this worthy battle. I provide more discussion on the professional and societal benefits of deploying the LV3 strategy as a *Transformational Leader* during this time in American history in the Epilogue.

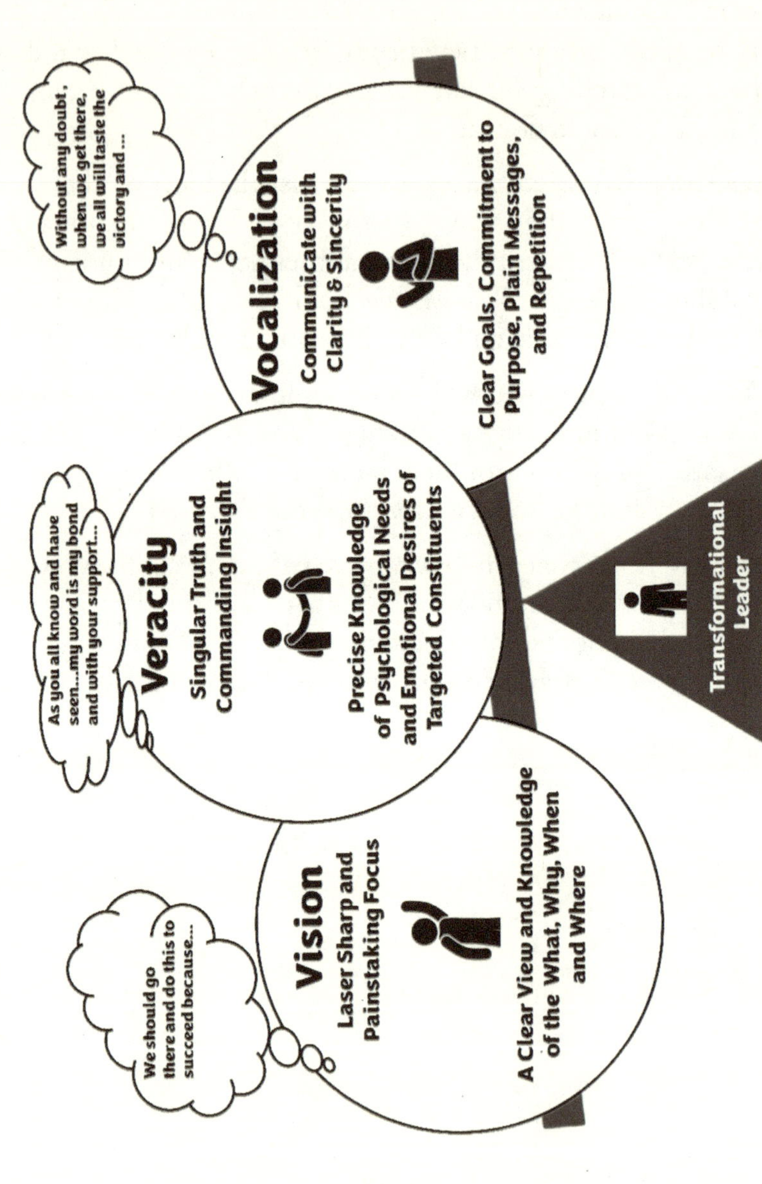
We should go there and do this to succeed because...
Vision
Laser Sharp and Painstaking Focus
A Clear View and Knowledge of the What, Why, When and Where
As you all know and have seen....my word is my bond and with your support...
Veracity
Singular Truth and Commanding Insight
Precise Knowledge of Psychological Needs and Emotional Desires of Targeted Constituents
Without any doubt, when we get there, we all will taste the victory and ...
Vocalization
Communicate with Clarity & Sincerity
Clear Goals, Commitment to Purpose, Plain Messages, and Repetition
Transformational Leader
Leveraging Vision, Veracity and Vocalization (LV3) Communications Strategy

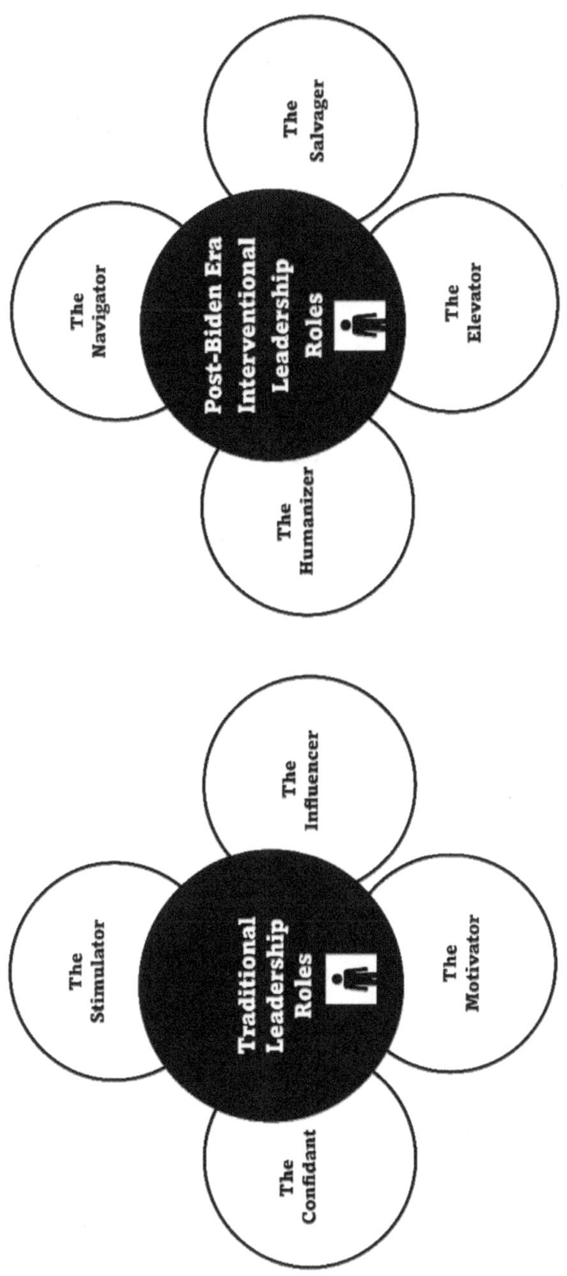

Eight Roles of Effective Transformational Leaders

"The greatest leaders are not necessarily those who do the greatest things. They are the ones that get people to do the greatest things."

– Ronald Reagan
American politician and act or who served as the 40th president of the United States.

CHAPTER TWO

Transformations and the Leadership Advantage

"Change is inevitable, but transformation is by conscious choice."
— Heather Amara

IN THIS BOOK'S INTRODUCTION, I discussed some of the "transformative results" that we take for granted in the 21st century that became a reality through the effective use of the *transformative leadership style.* These brilliant and sometimes heroic feats of ingenuity and determination did much more than just *change* the course of history. They clearly *transformed* human life on planet earth, as we know it today.

Also, as you may recall, I shared the following in the Introduction to Chapter One:

> *"I believe that this country's long and rich history, strongly suggests a Transformational Leadership focus and skillset, which is more aligned with shaping a new democratic-leaning future, supported by an unflappable plurality of Americans, and targeting the "real-world," twenty-first century challenges — and* **not**, *just an attempt, to put the* **genie**, *that escaped on November 5th, 2024, back in the bottle."*

The difference between my proposition of shaping a *democratic-leaning future* versus *putting the genie back in the bottle*, is the significant difference between *leading a change* versus *leading a transformation.*

As an overview for some and a reminder for others, let me first discuss the significant difference between a *change* and a *transformation.* Then, I will share some insights regarding the unique *advantage* that the discipline of *leadership* brings to the execution of initiatives whose impacts can result in generational improvements in productivity, humanity and civilization.

Change vs. Transformation

Change is doing things differently.	Transformation is a new way of being.

CHANGE INVOLVES INCREMENTAL, specific adjustments to existing systems or processes, while transformation is a more profound, fundamental shift that often involves reinventing or creating something new.

Change requires becoming familiar with the current situation, and working to make things better, faster, or cheaper. The past is the fundamental reference point and actions are intended to alter what already happened. The probability of a change initiative being successful is based on efficiencies and economies that are realized at the end of the effort, compared to the *"As Is"* situation prior to initiating the change activity.

The way I like to think about it, when you choose to change vs. to transform your future, you are choosing a future which is basically a *reconditioned* or *improved* version of the past.

On the other hand, a *transformation* is an affirmation that we desire the *actions* we do today to create our future tomorrow. In transformations, the nature, type, and size of the *actions* we take define and invent our future.

However, similar to a change, transformations also begin with firmly grasping and accepting the current state of affairs, or the "As Is." Without an honest and truthful understanding of the "As Is", we risk, from the outset, building our desired future upon a *flawed* foundation.

Below is a quick comparison of the major differences between a *change* and a *transformation.*

Changes vs. Transformations

The Goals	Changes make things better, faster, or more efficient.	Transformations redefine what success looks like and how to achieve it.
The Scopes	Changes are narrower, more incremental, and often focused on specific areas within an organization.	Transformations are broader, more extensive, and often involves a complete overhaul of the organization.
The Focuses	Change is focused on improving or modifying existing processes, systems, or practices.	Transformations are focused on reinventing the activity, changing core beliefs, values, and culture, and developing new ways.
The Timings	Changes may happen rapidly, but can also be a gradual process.	Transformations are typically a longer, more complex process.
The Motivations	Changes often a response to external pressures or internal inefficiencies.	Transformations are driven by a desire to create a new vision or address significant challenges.
Examples	Implementing new software to streamline a specific workflow is a change.	Shaping a new democratic-leaning future, supported by an unflappable plurality of Americans is a Transformation.
The Impacts	Changes typically affect a specific part of the entity or its processes.	Transformations often affect the whole entity, its culture, and its way of doing things.

I will discuss in the next section, why the significant breath, depth and complexity associated with leading *successful transformations* demand disciplined and skilled leaders.

The Leadership Advantage

IN PART ONE OF THIS BOOK, I share a personal perspective and those of other scholars and thought leaders regarding the unprecedented changes that have unfolded as a result of the November 2024 Presidential election. Of course, the major change has been our country's recent "pivot" away from over 230 years of democratic governance and toward a more autocratic-leading Federal government.

Within that context, I described in detail the "expansion" of the roles that *Transformational Leaders* must play as they successfully lead major transformations, and as they assume an important role in strengthening America's democratic-leaning culture in the Post-Biden era.

However, I have not, up until this point, addressed the true *elephants in the room* when it comes to the effectiveness of deploying the *Transformational Leadership* style. Not surprisingly, many of you are most likely aware of these *metaphorical elephants*, which are the *Leaders* themselves, and their ability to take full advantage of the inherent powers of the discipline of *Leadership.*

In Part Two of this book, I address both the *Leaders* and the discipline of *Leadership* that fuels and sustains the most successful transformational accomplishments. This part of the book is also intended to be a *primer* for many of you, and a reference guide to the process of maximizing, what I call *"The Leadership Advantage."*

As I researched the fundamentals of leadership development earlier in my career, I spent quite a bit of time simply asking individuals from all walks in life this question:

"What comes first to your mind when you hear the word leadership?"

I was not surprised to learn that most people think of leadership in terms of *people* or *groups of people* namely our *leadership team,* or the specific application of leadership knowledge and skills such as *the leadership process.*

The other thing that rang consistently true was that almost everyone I asked emphasized the need for an effective leader to have faithful followers, to be able to articulate a purpose or mission, and to know what is to be achieved or earned when victory is won. Yet, no one mentioned the need for an effective leader to *first* be an effective leader of his or herself.

In addition, in Part Two, I explore the concept of *"leading yourself"* and why leadership is truly a "verb" and a powerful professional competency; All anchored by what I call the *Absolute Attributes, which* innately touch every aspect of our lives and our relationships.

The concise discussions and explorations of the timeless perspectives in Part Two of this book build upon the premise that by strengthening a *primary set* of leadership attributes, any leader can gain an advantage over those who think of *leadership* as something that others do or merely as a process.

Today, I firmly believe that the proper grasp of these unique perspectives, and the strategic use of the *primary attributes* will become the *Leadership Advantage* of *Transformational Leaders,* as they lead major transformations, meet their client's expectations, and do it in such a manner that the byproduct will positively affect America's democratic-leaning culture in the Post-Biden era.

PART TWO
THE LEADERSHIP ADVANTAGE

PART TWO
THE LEADERSHIP ADVANTAGE

IN THE FOLLOWING TEN CHAPTERS, I will explore several distinctive perspectives on leadership. This more expansive way of viewing leadership and situationally adapting a core set of intrinsic leadership attributes can help all of us improve our professional performance and success in many aspects of our lives.

From this perspective, you will quickly begin to view leadership as a *verb* and appreciate its power as a strategic professional competency. Exploring this concept will expand your understanding and your ability to consciously employ the intrinsic human traits which embody "leadership" in its most complete form, that I call the *Ten Absolute Attributes of Leadership.*

Just as a verb is the most important part of a sentence, leadership can become the most important part of influencing the activities required to accomplish important goals in both your personal and professional life. *Leading is not something you observe. Leading is something you do.*

As mentioned in Chapter Two, this broader perspective of leadership and the strategic use of your *primary leadership attributes* will become your *Leadership Advantage.* As you gain this prospective, I contend that you will come to appreciate what millions of very successful leaders have learned, that is, *"Leadership is omnipresent."*

Each of the following chapters will give you the opportunity to closely explore one of the *Ten Absolute Attributes of Leadership,* and how they can influence and shape the most desired and most successful outcomes.

Before we began our exploration, let's first briefly examine the centuries old concept of leader traits and attributes and overview the practical method by which *The Ten Absolute Attributes* were selected from among dozens of documented leadership traits.

Leader Traits and Attributes

A TRAIT, OF COURSE, is what we call a characteristic way in which an individual perceives, feels, believes and acts. An attribute is an inherent characteristic or quality.

For centuries, pioneers of the field of human psychology and personality assessment have documented the most important leadership traits of their times based on theories, studies and observations. During your academic studies you most likely have come across many such lists of leadership attributes. Perhaps you have also studied the works of Erik Erikson, Abraham Maslow, Hans Eysenck, Robert White, Sigmond Freud, Albert Bandura and Carl Rogers. From Erikson's stages of psychosocial development to Maslow's famous theories of motivation to Rogers humanistic approach to personality, they all put forward their contemporary explanation of observations and behaviors. The question of how leaders differ from non-leaders is one of the oldest in psychology, yet it remains a source of disagreement and controversy among leadership scholars today.

In academia and contemporary literature, there are those who believe that leaders are born. This group is convinced that there are certain leadership attributes that are natural qualities possessed by only a very few people. While others believe that most people who do not naturally possess these leadership qualities can acquire them through diligent training and self-control.

In my studies of leaders and leadership traits over the past 30 years, as a student, a corporate executive and a teacher, it appears that with the exception of a few mega personalities who stand out above the rest, most leaders cling to a somewhat traditional set of widely touted leadership attributes or qualities.

Whether inherent or acquired, they tend to employ a specific set of attributes in a fashion similar to someone they have known, read about or admire. I am sure you can easily recognize the most common of these leadership attributes. Depending on a particular type of organization, environment or circumstance, a typical set of attributes would most likely include:

- Honesty, Responsibility, Confidence, and Enthusiasm
- Motivation, Reliability, Decisiveness, and Determination
- As well as, Loyalty and Courage.

All of which are admirable and sound human traits.

Although research shows that the possession of certain attributes alone does not guarantee leadership success, there is evidence that the most effective and enduring leaders do differ from other leaders in at least one obvious way. It appears that the most effective leaders have a distinct advantage in the ease in which they deploy their strongest leadership attributes. They also seem to consistently achieve both personal and professional success. They tend to get more leadership opportunities, win more of the battles in the trenches and earn more recognition, acknowledgment, respect and rewards.

How do they do this? What comprises their primary set of leadership attributes? Why does there appear to be a very strong relationship between their personal achievements and their professional achievements? What anchors the apparent trust, confidence and absoluteness when it comes to selecting, adapting and deploying certain leadership attributes?

These and other pertinent questions will be addressed in the following chapters as we continue our exploration of the *Leadership Advantage.*

The Ten Absolute Attributes of Leadership

WHILE PONDERING many of the questions presented in the previous section and reviewing dozens of studies, articles and research reports, I finally was able to generate a list of thirty-seven leadership attributes which appeared most often in published literature. I closely examined and ranked each attribute based on what my research and my real-world experience supported as the human traits most fundamental and absolute when it comes to effective 21st century leadership. At that point, I reduced the list down to the top ten attributes.

Although many other traits have been associated with successful and effective leaders, those selected as the *Ten Absolute Attributes of Leadership* are as follows:

- ¤ Presence
- ¤ Vision
- ¤ Clarity
- ¤ Persistence
- ¤ Motivation
- ¤ Unselfishness
- ¤ Deliberation
- ¤ Courage
- ¤ Respect; and
- ¤ Focus.

While all of the attributes studied could be described as worthy leadership traits, it was found that there were a couple of very distinctive and significant facets regarding this particular set of attributes as compared to most of the others.

First, each of the *Ten Absolute Attributes of Leadership* seems to encompass an inherent human characteristic that most people possess to some extent. Each of the attributes seems to find its way, at some point, into every professional's *successful leader* toolkit. Each attribute represents a distinct personal trait. Each trait is capable of being strengthened, lessened and even discounted based on the value an individual places on its innate existence and the situations, environments and circumstances encountered through his or her life.

As professionals...

- ¤ We all have some level of presence. When we walk into a room, we will be noticed.
  However, do we always know by whom and to what degree?

- We all depend on a plan, a road map or a vision to know what to do next or what to expect at the end of a journey.

  But, how broad and how deep is our visioning and can it be effectively communicated to others?

- We have all learned that a significant part of being viewed as a professional depends on our ability to clearly express ourselves verbally and in writing.

  But, then again, does our clarity present itself as sufficiently lucent and transparent when the situation demands it?

- We all have exhibited a level of persistence in order to have achieved our current position in life.

  But, how closely is our "dogged persistence" tied to long-term and trusted endurance?

- We all have been motivated by something or someone at multiple points in our lives and our careers.

  However, does the impetus of our motivation come with a lot of overhead and can it be easily translated into a source for stimulating others?

- We all have learned that being an effective team member requires a degree of compromise and unselfishness.

  But, can we always balance what may be perceived as unselfishness or bigheartedness with what can also be interpreted as a weakness?

- We all have some ability to be thoughtful and deliberate.

  But, how can we prevent "too much deliberation" or the lack of deliberation from negatively impacting our ability to reach our goals.

- We all have some mental or moral strength to persevere and withstand danger, fear, or difficulty.

  However, because courage is required in almost every basic human activity or endeavor, how do we ration our courageousness consistent with the results that can be expected?

¤ We all desire to be respected and we understand its value in getting things done through others.

But, are we capable of consistently giving the proper level of respect to situations and circumstances as well as to individuals?

¤ We all have some ability to direct our attention to events and activities when it is apparent that there is a need or a problem.

However, do we have the natural instinct or sufficient skill to proactively plant strategic and tactical markers to ensure that the proper focus is always where it needs to be?

The second distinctive and significant facet regarding this particular set of attributes is the realization that collectively, they embody what many people in today's business world are seeking in a leader; both as a superior and as a person.

Most of today's contemporary literature describes an effective leader as someone who is not only capable of inspiring others but also has the attributes required to cultivate a broad and deep level of trust throughout an organization. He or she must also be competent at coordinating and collaborating among the many different and diverse resources which reside throughout the organization. When a leader possesses a strong combination and a high degree of personal attributes such as presence, clarity, unselfishness and respectfulness, he or she will find it significantly easier to cultivate trust and rely on others.

The understanding of the *collective significance* of these ten attributes combined with the recognition that most of us possess all these inherent human characteristics, to some extent, makes the opportunity of gaining a *Leadership Advantage* available to all of us.

I would suggest that the probability of any one being born with what might be considered a *maximum level* of all ten attributes is fairly small.

However, most professionals who have achieved a leadership position most likely possess at least an *average level* of all ten of these attributes. As illustrated in the diagram on the next page, by increasing your innate levels of each attribute, you can elevate yourself to a higher position on the opportunity scale. This increase in position should also equate to an increase in *Leadership Advantage.*

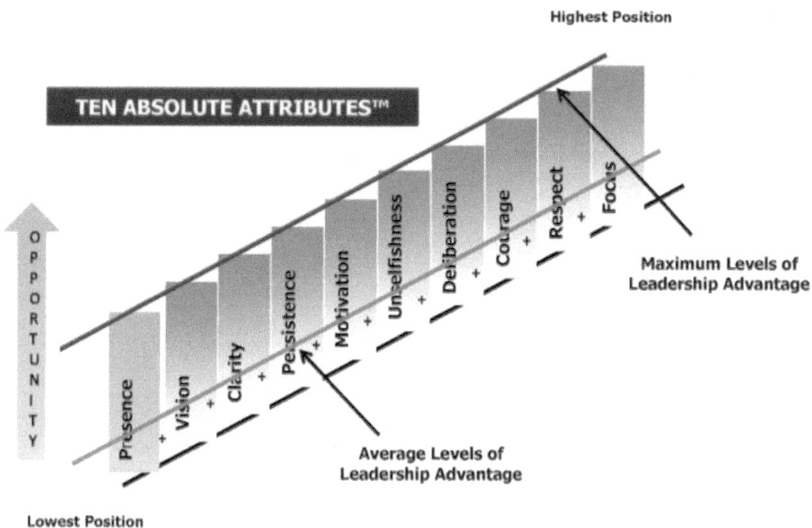

In the following chapters we explore opportunities for increasing innate levels of each *Absolute Attribute* and provide specific insight into the personal and professional goals you should pursue to allow each of the *Ten Absolute Attributes* to play its role in helping you maximize your *Leadership Advantage.*

CHAPTER THREE
LEADERSHIP AND **PRESENCE**

LEADERSHIP AND **PRESENCE**

AS PROFESSIONALS, we all have some level of *presence.* When we walk into a room, we will be noticed. However, do we always know by whom and to what degree? In order to gain a better understanding of how the traits associated with your *presence,* as an individual and a leader, influences outcomes and what you can do to enhance your innate presence, we will explore the following:

- What is *presence* and why it is a major factor when it comes to successfully *leading yourself* and leading others?
- How can you develop or enhance your command of *presence?* and
- What is the primary role of *presence* in establishing and maintaining a leadership advantage?

The Power of Presence

PERSONAL PRESENCE is not easy to define, but we all know it when we see it. Everyone notices it when you walk into a room. Almost on cue, heads turn, and people step aside. Regardless of the subject being discussed, the conversation opens up to include you. When you speak everyone listens. When you ask a question, someone is always there with an answer.

The same is true with what can be called *leadership presence.* Leadership presence can be thought of as the ability to do at least a couple of things very well. The first is to demonstrate your worth, whether to one person or to hundreds of thousands of people, in an authentic way. The second is to connect well with your stakeholders. This requires being authentic, comfortable in your own skin and being able to get your message across to everyone who should find it important.

Like the adage, "charity starts at home", developing a strong command of our leadership presence also starts at home. Because presence is the radiance of authenticity, it's a major factor when it comes to leading yourself and leading others.

Home is the place where we radiate the most sincerity and learn what it takes to make good things happen on a consistent basis. Leading ourselves to recognize and appreciate "presence", starts with recognizing and appreciating who we are as an individual and as a leader.

As a business or organization leader in today's environment of global commerce and social media, you have literally hundreds of interpersonal interactions each day. If at any time you fail to instill confidence among subordinates and peers, you may lose their loyalty, harm their morale and hinder their ability to execute.

The impact, reach and power of presence is not only limited to your co-workers, but to everyone with whom you come in contact with throughout the day and every day. Your presence or lack thereof, as an individual and a leader, can be a major factor in your relationships at work and at home.

You should remember that your *presence* is an *Absolute Attribute.* That is, presence is vital to what completes you as an individual. Your personal presence feeds your professional presence and they both come from within and are under your control. By strategically elevating your leadership presence and using it in concert with your other *Absolute Attributes*, you can take your influence as a leader to a whole, new level.

Enhancing Command of Presence

SOME LEADERS HAPPEN upon the skill of commanding their presence naturally, while others have to work very hard to develop it. While there are many things that lead to developing a strong "command presence", a focus on developing the following three areas will have an immediate impact on enhancing your command presence.

1. Be Trustworthy and Show People You Care

When you closely examine the characteristics of what really constitutes effective leadership and distinguishes truly effective leaders from all others, you will find that it is not power, not a title, not authority or not even technical competency.

Instead, what sets you apart is your ability to earn and keep both the loyalty and trust of those whom you lead. Strong leadership presence will allow you to easily project your trust worthiness, your humility and your concern for the welfare of others.

When you take the time to build strong relationships with those you lead, you can more easily earn their trust and loyalty. This sort of human and business connection will allow you to span positional and philosophical gaps, survive mistakes, challenges, downturns and other obstacles that will inevitably occur.

2. Develop Great Verbal Skills

As you are most likely aware, you began developing great verbal skills by developing great listening skills. You must try to understand before you can be understood. When it is time to speak, you should say what you mean and mean what you say. What you say, when you say it, and how you say it will either spawn confidence as well as serve to motivate and inspire, or it will take the wind right out of your sails. It is not necessary to be long-winded. You should just be measured and articulate. Remember, that as the leader, a "whisper" may be perceived by some subordinates as a "roar". It is very difficult to lead if you cannot communicate with clarity and with ease.

3. Making Good Decisions

Nothing is more detrimental for you as a leader than a poor track record. Your ability to layer a solid decision upon solid decision is crucial to creating loyalty. Making good decisions not only instills confidence. It is also the best way to lead. Your track record of good decisions is an example for those you lead. A track record of making good decisions does not take long to become part of your reputation, which provides you with a heightened level of trust, respect and leadership presence even prior to entering a room.

The bottom line is that if you develop a strong command presence, becoming a more effective and admired leader becomes easier.

Presence and the Leadership Advantage

PRESENCE IS A UNIQUE competence and fundamental to the concept of Leadership *Advantage*. As we all know, competence is best defined as possessing the skill and knowledge required to *take the action* necessary to ensure successful outcomes. Competence also describes our ability to apply prior experience to new situations with good results. The competency associated with your presence usually increases over time as you acquire more life experience.

Presence is the leadership attribute which creates the groundwork necessary to maximize the influence of all the other *Absolute Attributes*. A strong case can be made that once you are viewed as having a strong professional presence; meaning, being in the moment, possessing numerous positive relationships throughout your organization, perceived as being a passionate communicator and a truly authentic individual; maximizing the influence of the other nine *Absolute Attributes* becomes a much easier task.

With a strong command of your presence, your *vision* is better understood. Your written and verbal communications take on a special level of *clarity*. Your *persistence* becomes contagious. Your ability to *motivate* others becomes effortless.

The following chart summarizes the personal goals you should pursue to enable *presence* to play a role in helping you maximize your *Leadership Advantage*.

Average Level of Presence	Maximum Level of Presence
You respond to most situations in a consistent and familiar manner; or	**You act in the moment and you are flexible enough to handle the unexpected.**
You allow your relationships to develop based on the individual and perceived value to you; or	**You build relationships through empathy, listening and authentic connections.**
You convey most of your messages with clarity and clear authority; or	**You express feelings and emotions while delivering one congruent message.**
You adjust your responses and actions based on who you are around; or	**You accept yourself, you are authentic, and you reflect your values in your actions.** ***This is your Leadership Advantage***

CHAPTER FOUR
LEADERSHIP AND **VISION**

LEADERSHIP AND **VISION**

WE ALL DEPEND on a plan, a road map or a vision to know what to do next or what to expect at the end of a journey. But, how broad and how deep is our visioning and can it be effectively communicated to others?

In order to explore the relationship between "leadership" and "vision" and reveal possible opportunities for a *leadership advantage*, we must remove ourselves from the idea that all leaders have vision and that the very essence of leadership is to have the ability to articulate a vision.

By removing ourselves from this fundamentally sound but practically suspect premise, we are left with the need to start our exploration by taking a closer look at the art of visioning and then gaining a broader view of how this powerful attribute can be practically deployed beyond simply sharing a dream or painting a picture for others.

So, let's briefly explore:

¤ What is the art of visioning and why do some do it better than others?

¤ How can you leverage this attribute beyond telling a passionate story?

¤ What advantage you will gain by becoming a more skilled "visioneer" in all aspects of your life?

The Art of Visioning

DURING HIS 1992 presidential re-election campaign, President George H. W. Bush alluded to how he did not know what "the vision-thing" was all about. He lost. In contrast, his opponent said that he had a clear vision of a revitalized America. He won.

While it is certain that vision is not the whole story, the outcome re-affirmed the wisdom of Proverbs 29:18*: "Where there is no vision, the people perish."* I believe that this is true of any undertaking where the hearts and minds of others, as well as yourself, are the most important ingredients of success. But, as we shall see in this chapter, a vision is more than the inspiration of a visionary leader. Your vision must also include the details of execution that create clear direction and understanding. This is why I also believe that visioning is an art.

Most dictionaries define vision as the *"power of discerning future conditions; shrewdness in planning and foresight."* To some extent, we all have such power. Some of us are more inherently capable than others of looking into the future, whether it is next year or next week and plan for certain outcomes. However, the main challenge associated with successfully achieving your "visions" is not the lack of inherent visionary capability. Rather, it is about understanding and acquiring the skills of articulating and leveraging this important leadership attribute to your advantage.

The art of visioning enables us to move forward with clarity. It links the specific business or personal objectives and targets with our core values. The process also helps us to define a plan that we can use to guide us to successfully achieving our goals. It is a process that speaks directly to the need for an inspiring yet detailed vision for both professional, personal and civil success.

The following six steps provide a framework for touching most of the bases associated with crafting a vision to help guide you through a current business or personal situation.

1. **Capture the Current Situation**

   Where are you today and where do you need to be in the future? In this step you should not ignore what is happening around you today nor should you work in isolation. Utilize friends, acquaintances and family members to help you honestly gain an awareness of your present state. Your appraisal should include all of the advantages and disadvantages.

2. **Define the Best Outcome**

   What can you expect to achieve? In this step, it is important to evaluate all of your options based on a "realistic" assessment. Then, select the best outcome that can be realized with the level of risk you are willing to accept. This selection will translate into your goal and where you expect to land when all is said and done. It is, in effect, your *vision.*

3. **Embrace the Importance of the Outcome**

   Why is this important to you? At times, we may create a vision for ourselves or our organization which is more of a fad or something you must do because everyone else is doing it. Defining a vision or goal without understanding and truly embracing why it is important to you or your organization is meaningless.

4. **Determine the Obstacles to Achieving Success**

   Who or what is in your way? Determining what you need or where you want to be, can be a success in its own right. However, knowing how to get there and doing it is the ultimate challenge. It is useful to identify in a proactive manner the possible obstacles that you foresee in the way to achieving your vision. These obstacles may be geographic, may be related to people or to financial resources or even environmental factors that could adversely impact your actions.

5. Determine the Actions to Overcome all Obstacles

What will you do and when? This is a crucial step. Identifying the appropriate and available actions required to reach your vision is paramount to your success. Determining the changes that are clearly within your control and can be initiated early is very important. Selecting a set of actions that are "appropriate" and "available" is the most important part of the execution. Otherwise, without them the vision remains a dream.

6. Set Priorities and Monitor Result

Have you properly laid the groundwork for the next set of actions? Are you on track to achieve your ultimate goal? It is tempting to try to change everything at once. Prudence dictates that you work on the basis of defined priorities. Without priorities, you could squander valuable resources, time and effort in working on relatively less important actions. You should monitor your results against stated actions and track your progress towards achieving your vision.

Leverage Visioning Beyond Passionate Storytelling

OVER THE YEARS, I have discovered that there are two elements common to all effective visions: 1) they are all implemented, and 2) they all yield the planned results. This is true regardless of whether the vision targets professional or personal goals.

As I mentioned earlier, leadership has many definitions and many valuable components or attributes. *Vision* has been selected as one the *Absolute Attributes* in the context of the Leadership Advantage for four primary reasons. When we subject ourselves to the art of the visioning process, we go beyond enhancing our professional ability to tell a good story. We also ignite our personal and natural tendencies for *reflection*, *socialization*, *experimentation* and *observation*.

Here are some thoughts to keep in mind around the power of visioning in connection with your Leadership Advantage.

- **Reflection** - A vision of any type can only be developed when you take time away to reflect and slow down.
- **Socialization** - The planning and execution of a vision must involve others for two reasons. First, none of us are fully self-sufficient. We are, as humans, built to be interdependent on one another. Second, we have a hard time seeing what is exceptional within us and we need others to point that out.
- **Experimentation** - Visions that have tangible, positive and lasting results are cultivated when we experiment within our areas of interests and gifting. We learn more about ourselves by doing.
- **Observation** - Honing a professional or personal vision requires good self-awareness and tracking our responses to the various experiments we conduct.

The Advantages of Becoming a Skilled "Visioneer"

THERE ARE ADVANTAGES you can gain by becoming a more skilled visioneer in all aspects of your life. Here are just a few:

- Visioning is the first step in crafting strategic and achievable plans for your career, family and life.
- A well-crafted vision that is shared by all the members of your family and/or your business or company can help everyone involved to assist in the advancement and achievement of your goals.
- A vision brings meaning to what you do every day. It can mobilize others to support you with action and not just words.
- A vision can grab people and then bring them into the fold.

As a skilled visioner, you are able to craft effective visions. An effective vision strikes a chord in people. It motivates them by tapping their competitive drive. It arouses desire for greatness or interest in doing the right thing. It tantalizes them with personal gain. It appeals to their need to make a difference in the world. When your vision is effective and strong, all of your stakeholders get caught up in what you are doing. They absorb the vision, and commit themselves to your goals and your values.

The following chart summarizes the personal goals you should pursue to enable *vision* to play a role in helping you maximize your *Leadership Advantage*.

Average Level of Vision	Maximum Level of Vision
You quickly sense your situation without a thorough review; or	**You take the time to capture all aspects of the situation.**
You assume that the outcome is the best available to you; or	**You define the best outcome and know why it is important to you and your goals.**
You do what you feel is necessary and hope everything works out; or	**You identify the appropriate and available actions required to reach your vision.**
You take advantage of the opportunities that surface to move you toward your goals; or	**You set priorities, monitor results closely and lay the groundwork for the next set of actions.** ***This is your Leadership Advantage***

"For those who confuse you, recognize that their confusion is theirs and your clarity is yours."

— Barbara Marciniak
Inspirational speaker and best-selling author

CHAPTER FIVE

LEADERSHIP AND **CLARITY**

LEADERSHIP AND **CLARITY**

WE ALL HAVE LEARNED that a significant part of being viewed as a professional depends on our ability to clearly express ourselves verbally and in writing. Both verbal and written communications are essential for effective business and personal expression. Clarity leads to effective communication.

While there are many subtleties to verbal communication between people, some basic skills can help you leverage this key attribute to become a more effective communicator. In order to have achieved the success you have achieved in both your personal and professional life, you are most likely already a good communicator. I have found that we all can improve the *clarity* of our communications in any situation by becoming more cognizant of some natural communications barriers.

These barriers fall into the following camps:

- Barriers to Listening;
- Barriers to Accurate Perception; and
- Barriers to Effective Verbal Communication

In this chapter we will explore these three barriers as well as some suggested strategies for effectively addressing them.

Barriers to Listening

THE FOLLOWING are examples of some barriers to listening which tend to interfere with the clarity of our communications. They are actions or situations that you should be keenly aware of and development methods to eliminate and/or control. I have also included a list of strategies that can be used to effectively assist in overcoming such barriers.

- **Focusing on a Personal Agenda**

When we spend our listening time formulating our next response, we cannot be fully attentive to what the speaker is saying.

- **Experiencing Information Overload**

Too much stimulation or information can make it very difficult to listen with full attention. You should try to focus on the relevant information and the central points that are being conveyed.

- **Criticizing the Speaker**

You should not be distracted by critical evaluations of the speaker. You should make every attempt to focus on what the speaker is saying or the message rather than the messenger.

- **Getting Distracted by Emotional Noise**

All of us naturally react emotionally to certain words, concepts and ideas, and to a myriad of other cues from speakers (including appearance and non-verbal cues). You should make a conscious effort to quiet your own emotional reactions so that you can listen and respond properly.

- **Getting Distracted by External Noise**

Audible noise may be extremely distracting. Some things can be minimized, such as turning down the ringer on your phone and the sounds on your computer while meeting with someone.

- **Experiencing Physical Difficulty**

Feeling physically ill or experiencing pain can make it very difficult to listen effectively. You may wish to communicate that this is not a good time and reschedule the discussion.

Otherwise, you may just need to concentrate even more on the task of listening.

STRATEGIES FOR OVERCOMING BARRIERS TO LISTENING

Stop. You should focus on the other person, their thoughts and feelings. Try to consciously focus on quieting your own internal commentary and step away from your own concerns to think about those of the speaker. Give your full attention to the speaker.

Look. You should pay attention to non-verbal messages, without letting yourself be distracted. Notice body language and non-verbal cues to allow for a richer understanding of the speaker's point. However, avoid getting distracted from the verbal message.

Listen. You should listen to the essence of the speaker's thoughts, details, major ideas and their meanings. Seek an overall understanding of what the speaker is trying to communicate, rather than reacting to the individual words or terms that they use to express themselves.

Be Empathetic. You should try to imagine how you would feel if you were in their circumstances. Be empathetic to the feelings of the speaker, while maintaining a calm center within you. You need not be drawn into all of their problems or issues, as long as you acknowledge what they are experiencing.

Ask Questions. You should use questions to clarify your understanding, as well as to demonstrate interest in what is being said.

Barriers to Accurate Perception

THE FOLLOWING are examples of some barriers to you obtaining an accurate perception of someone or a situation. I have also included a list of strategies that can be used to effectively assist in overcoming such barriers.

- **Stereotyping and Generalizing**

  Be careful not to hold on to preconceptions about people or things. We often tend to see what we want to see, forming an impression from a small amount of information or one experience and assuming that to be highly representative of the whole person or situation.

- **Not Investing Time**

  Making assumptions and ignoring details or circumstances can lead to misconceptions. When we fail to look in-depth for causes or circumstances, we miss important details and do not allow for the complexity of the situation.

- **Having a Distorted Focus**

  Focusing on the negative aspects of a conversation or a situation is a habit common to many of us. Even though we may recognize the positive things, we often give more weight to the negative, allowing one negative comment to overshadow numerous positive ones.

- **Assuming Similar Interpretations**

  Not everyone will draw the same conclusions from a given situation or set of information. Everybody interprets things differently. Make sure to check for other people's interpretations and be explicit about your own.

- **Experiencing Incongruent Cues**

  As speakers, and as listeners, we are constantly and simultaneously sending cues and receiving them from other people. You should try to be consistent with your verbal cues and your body language. You should refrain from saying one thing and expressing something else through your body language. You should be aware of how your non-verbal communication relates to your spoken words. If someone else seems to be sending a double message -- by saying one thing and expressing something else in their body language -- ask for clarification.

STRATEGIES FOR OVERCOMING BARRIERS TO ACCURATE PERCEPTION

Analyze Your Own Perceptions. You should question your perceptions, and think about how they are formed. Check in with others around you regularly and be aware of the assumptions that you are making. You can also seek additional information and observations. You may just need to ask people if your perceptions are accurate.

Work on Improving Your Perception. One way to do this is to increase your awareness of barriers to perception and which ones you tend towards. You should check in with yourself regularly. Seek honest, constructive feedback from others regarding their perceptions of you as a means of increasing your self-awareness.

Focus on Others. You should develop your ability to focus on other people and understand them better by trying to gather knowledge about them, listening to them actively, and imagining how you would feel in their situation.

Barriers to Effective Verbal Communication

THERE ARE MANY obvious and not so obvious barriers to verbal communication and these may occur at any stage in the communication process. Barriers may lead to your message becoming distorted. Effective verbal communication involves overcoming these barriers and conveying a clear and concise message. The following are examples of such barriers. I have also included a list of strategies that can be used to effectively assist in overcoming them.

- **Lacking Clarity**

  You should avoid all abstract, overly formal language, colloquialisms and jargon, which obscure your message more than they serve to impress people.

- **Stereotyping Complex Systems or Situations**

  Leaders and speakers who make unqualified generalizations undermine their own clarity and leadership. Be careful not to get stuck in the habit of using stereotypes or generalizing about complex systems or situations. Another form of generalization is "polarization" or creating extremes. Try to be sensitive to the complexities of situations, rather than viewing the world in black and white.

- **Jumping to Conclusions**

  Confusing facts with inferences is a common tendency. Do not assume you know the reasons behind events or that certain facts necessarily have certain implications. Make sure you have all the information you can get and then speak clearly about the facts versus the meanings or interpretations you attach to those.

- **Dysfunctional Responses**

  Ignoring or not responding to a comment or question quickly undermines effective communication. Likewise, responding with an irrelevant comment; one that is not connected to the topic at hand; will quash genuine communication. Interrupting others while they are speaking also creates a poor environment for communication.

- **Lacking Confidence**

  Lacking confidence can be a major barrier to effective communication and clarity. Shyness, difficulty being assertive or lack of self-worth can hinder your ability to make your needs and opinions known. Also, a lack of awareness of your own rights and opportunities in a given situation can prevent you from expressing your needs openly.

STRATEGIES FOR EFFECTIVE VERBAL COMMUNICATION

Focus on the Issue, Not the Person. You should try not to take everything personally, and similarly, express your own needs and opinions in terms of the job at hand. Solve problems rather than attempt to control others. For example, rather than criticizing a co-worker's personality, express your concerns in terms of how to get the job done more smoothly in the future.

Be Genuine. You should be yourself, authentic, honest and open. Be honest with yourself and focus on working well with the people around you and acting with integrity.

Empathize. Although professional relationships with others entail some boundaries when it comes to interaction with colleagues, it is important to demonstrate sensitivity and to really care about the people you work with. If you do not care about them, it will be difficult for them to care about you when it comes to working together.

Be Flexible. You should allow for other points of view, and be open to other ways of doing things. Diversity brings creativity and innovation.

Value Your Own Experiences. You should be firm about your own rights, desires and needs. Undervaluing yourself encourages others to undervalue you, too. Offer your ideas and expect to be treated well.

Present Yourself as an Equal. Even when you are in a position of authority, focus on what you and the other person each have to offer and to contribute to the job or issue.

Use Affirming Responses. Respond to others in ways that acknowledge their experiences. Thank them for their input. Affirm their right to their feelings, even if you disagree. Ask questions, express positive feeling and provide positive feedback when possible.

The following chart summarizes the personal goals you should pursue to enable *Clarity* to play a role in helping you maximize your *Leadership Advantage.*

Average Level of Clarity	Maximum Level of Clarity
You are aware that there are communication barriers, however you have not taken any actions to identify them ; or	You have identified your primary barriers to effective listening and communicating.
You address communication barriers when you are faced with them; or	You develop specific and actionable strategies to address perceived barriers prior to all major communications.
You address what might appear as inaccurate perceptions doing the "heat of the moment" and hope things work out; or	You are aware of the most effective strategies to overcome perception barriers and you deploy them as required.
You depend on your intuition to guide you around communication barriers; or	You have developed the skills required to positively navigate through the most common barriers to communication. *This is your Leadership Advantage*

CHAPTER SIX
LEADERSHIP AND PERSISTENCE

"Patience, persistence and perspiration make an unbeatable combination for success."

–Napoleon Hill

American author in the area of the new thought movement.

LEADERSHIP AND **PERSISTENCE**

WE ALL HAVE EXHIBITED a level of persistence in order to have achieved our current position in life. Persistence is the quality that allows us to continue doing something or trying to do something even though it is difficult or maybe opposed by others.

Persistence is a quality that we, as leaders, should all nurture and view as an advantage that can be utilized in both our professional and personal lives.

Your ability to hold on or to get back up after you have been knocked down has been essential for the success you have achieved. As we all know, there will be failures along the way and it is your level and use of this important *Absolute Attribute* that will help you turn failures into stepping stones to future successes.

Calvin Coolidge, 30th United States President, once said *"Nothing in the world can take the place of persistence. Talent will not; nothing is more common than unsuccessful men with talent. Genius will not; unrewarded genius is almost proverb. Education will not; the world is full of educated derelicts. Persistence and determination alone are omnipotent."*

As an *Absolute Attribute, Persistence* allows us to begin, do and finish. Persistence reinforces and strengthens all of the other *Absolute Attributes.*

Persistence is essential to being an effective leader as well as achieving your maximum Leadership Advantage.

However, in order to maintain and expand our natural levels of persistence, we all can benefit from some basic techniques which will increase our consciousness and sharpen our awareness of what makes us persistent.

In this chapter, we will briefly overview some of those techniques and highlight how you can leverage your business or organizational approaches by applying these techniques in all aspects of your professional, personal and civil life.

Face Problems Head On

IT IS NOT YOUR PROBLEMS that define you; it is how you react and recover from them. Your problems are not going away unless you do something about them. Facing problems in business and organizational settings tend to be an easier task as compared to your personal life. In these settings, as a leader, you have access to experts (finance, logistics, human resources, legal, etc.) who assist in defining the problem.

They also look to you to integrate the facts and realities and to lead them, and the organization, to successful outcomes. In other words, these external resources and organizational roles augment your innate level of persistence.

The key to gaining this Leadership Advantage in all aspects of your professional and personal life is approaching every problem not only "head on" but also with a strategy to utilize all of the internal and external expertise you can muster to tackle it. You will greatly benefit from the expanded level of insight, determination and persistence.

Be Passionate about What You Do

CHOOSING PROJECTS that you are passionate about makes being persistent more natural. But, if you go into something half-heartedly or because you feel obliged, the hard times seem harder.

If you continuously get stopped in an area and lack the motivation to continue, you should stop, take a close look and see what is going on. It might be that you are not really inspired by what you are doing or maybe you have just lost sight of the bigger picture of why you are doing what you are doing. In both your professional and personal life, there will be some projects, assignments or tasks that you get to choose and others that you do not get to choose.

Regardless of how the task at hand surfaced, the more passionate you are about getting it done, the more persistence you will be about achieving the desired outcome.

Be Honest to Yourself

BE HONEST ABOUT what you want to achieve, how you want to be perceived when it is accomplished and the obstacles that may prevent you from successfully executing a project, assignment or task. Just as being a fair and honest leader is critical to your long term professional success, being honest with yourself, in all aspects of your life, yields many long term benefits as well.

When you are striving to be the best that you can be, honesty has to be at the foundation. Honesty is the bridge to authenticity and self-compassion. Honesty allows you to set realistic goals. It bolsters your courage and unleashes your highest levels of confidence, determination, and persistence.

Choose your Battles Wisely

HAVE YOU EVER found yourself in the middle of a situation or challenge and suddenly come to the realization that you do not really want a particular goal as much as you once thought. You may end up choosing not to be persistent in that endeavor.

While *Persistence* is an *Absolute Attribute* that seems to always enhance all of the others, there are times when "less is better." If you find yourself in a situation where you are running into a brick wall over and over again and getting no closer to your goal, then persistence is not a good thing. It is vital here to figure out if you have chosen the best path to reach the goal.

Just as in your professional life, challenges in all aspects of your life require a way to weed out what is important to you and reprioritizing. It is important to determine whether the battle you have chosen is worthy of your "dogged persistence."

Remember the Reasons you want to reach your Goal

WHEN YOU FEEL your determination begin to waver, remember the reason you want to accomplish your goal. For most of us, the only goals we will succeed in reaching are those that are truly important to us. Keeping the reasons established for reaching a goal prominently in front of you is important to maintaining the level of persistence required to fully achieve the desired outcomes.

The chart on the following page summarizes the personal goals you should pursue to enable *Persistence* to play a role in helping you maximize your *Leadership Advantage.*

Average Level of Persistence	Maximum Level of Persistence
You tend to resist facing most problems head on unless they become unavoidable; or	You consciously take all problems head on and utilize all of the expertise you can muster to tackle them.
You are passionate about most of what you do, but sometimes find yourself taking on some tasks half-heartedly; or	You are always passionate about what you do in both your professional, personal and civil life.
You are sometimes not honest with yourself and find it difficult to maintain a high level of persistence doing some tasks; or	You are always honest with yourself in all aspects of your life. You strive to set realistic goals.
You do not choose your battles wisely and sometimes question if the task is worthy of your persistence; or	You choose your battles wisely and persist in all endeavors you undertake. *This is your Leadership Advantage*

CHAPTER SEVEN
LEADERSHIP AND MOTIVATION

LEADERSHIP AND **MOTIVATION**

WE ALL HAVE BEEN motivated by something or someone at multiple-points in our lives and our careers. But do we really know why? More importantly, if the motivator was in a leadership position, was the motivation due to inspiration or unrecognized coercion? A motivator is a person who makes others enthusiastic about doing something.

Unfortunately, enthusiasm could be the results of inspiration or coercion. The latter is usually short-lived and creates a new set of issues. An effective leader, on the other hand, is a person who guides or directs others. It is much easier to guide or direct someone who is motivated to follow you. Both good motivators and good leaders have the skills and training required to accomplish the desired outcomes, if they are to be successful.

However, I have found *motivational leadership* to be more of an art form. Good motivational leaders must first understand the art of motivation and how to use their innate motivational skills to implement a model and strategy that work for them as they guide and direct others. Too often many of us tend to believe that leadership skills are synonymous with motivational skills. Although there are some common components, there are also some distinct differences.

As an *Absolute Attribute*, *Motivation* is the ability to uplift and inspire people to perform at their best. However, in order to maximize your Leadership Advantage, you must leverage your motivational skills to motivate yourself to do what is required. Then, you should strive to be the kind of person that makes you the best motivational leader you can be. Both are necessary for maximum performance.

In this chapter we will explore four fundamental but imperative questions regarding motivation and how this broad reaching *Absolute Attribute* can contribute to maximizing your Leadership Advantage. They are:

- What is Motivation?
- What are the Components of Motivation?
- What can You do to Strengthen Your Motivation? and
- How to Lead and Motivate Yourself?

What is Motivation?

MOTIVATION IS DEFINED as the process that initiates, guides and maintains goal-oriented behaviors. Motivation is what causes us to act, whether it is getting a glass of water to reduce thirst or reading a book to gain knowledge.

Motivation involves the biological, emotional, social, and cognitive forces that activate behavior. In everyday usage, the term motivation is frequently used to describe why a person does something. For example, you might say that a student is so motivated to get into a leadership program that she spends every night studying.

The term motivation refers to factors that activate, direct and sustain goal-directed behavior. Motives are the "whys" of behavior; the needs or wants that drive behavior and explain what we do. We do not actually observe a motive. Rather, we infer that one exists based on the behavior we observe.

Psychologists have proposed a number of different theories of motivation, including drive theory, instinct theory, and humanistic theory. You should spend more time reviewing these intriguing theories to gain a better sense of their depth.

What are the Components of Motivation?

ANYONE WHO HAS EVER had a goal (like wanting to lose ten pounds or wanting to run a marathon) probably immediately realizes that simply having the desire to accomplish something is not enough. Achieving such a goal requires the ability to persist through obstacles and the endurance to keep going in spite of difficulties.

The two main components to motivation are *activation* and *persistence.*

- *Activation* involves the decision to initiate a behavior, such as enrolling in a leadership class.
- *Persistence* is the continued effort toward a goal even though obstacles may exist, such as taking more leadership courses in order to earn a degree although it requires a significant investment of time, energy, and resources.

There are two types of motivation, *extrinsic* and *intrinsic.* Here is a quick explanation and discussion on each of the two types.

Extrinsic Motivation

A PERSON IS EXTRINSICALLY motivated when the primary source of motivation is to attain a tangible outcome such as a reward, or to avoid a negative consequence such as a punishment. In a work setting, people are extrinsically motivated if the principal reason for their effort at work is pay, positive performance reviews, opportunities for advancement and bonuses.

Similarly, people are also extrinsically motivated if the principal reason for the effort at work is to avoid reprimands, poor performance reviews, poor assignments and dismissals. Notice that with extrinsic motivation, the source of motivation is external to the task itself. The tangible outcome we seek, such as a pay raise, is invariably administered (or controlled) by someone else.

Intrinsic Motivation

THE SECOND TYPE of motivation is intrinsic motivation. People are intrinsically motivated when the principal reason for their effort at work is that they find the work itself exciting, challenging, fulfilling, interesting and energizing. Furthermore, they get feelings of pride, feelings of achievement and feelings of accomplishment when working on these tasks.

What Can You Do to Strengthen Your Motivation?

MOTIVATION IS LIKE MUSCLE. You need to practice strengthening it through a regular routine. Here are some documented ways for increasing, maintaining and strengthening your motivation.

- **Set Small, Measurable Goals**.

  If you have a major goal, it would be a good idea if you split it into several minor goals with each small goal leading to your major goal. This way you will find it easier to motivate yourself. You will also not feel overwhelmed by the size of your goal and the things you have to do. This will also help you feel that the goal is more feasible and easier to accomplish.

- **Develop a Mantra.**

  A mantra is a verbal statement that reinforces a positive mindset. A mantra can be extremely helpful when it comes to keeping your motivation up and your spirits high. Come up with a statement that really resonates with you.

- **Face your Fears.**

  If pessimism is an obstacle to motivation, fear is the entire obstacle course. Fears come in all shapes and sizes. No matter what the fear, fear is one of the biggest reasons why people give up on their goals and dreams. What many fail to realize, however, is that on the other side of fear is confidence. While scary, facing your fears gives you a great sense of accomplishment and allows you to broaden your horizons. If you can tackle one small fear, what is to stop you from tackling a larger one?

- **Become a Good Mental Debater.**

  The journey to obtaining a goal has its peaks and valleys. In order to keep your motivation up, it is important to learn optimism. Believe it or not, optimism is a learned mental state. The first step to learning optimism is to acknowledge the moments when you are being pessimistic. Once they have been acknowledged, you have the power to debate pessimism away. Practice using a positive frame of mind to talk away all of your doubts and negative thoughts.

- **Visualize your Goals.**

  Goals can change and evolve day to day. However, if you create a great visualization of what it will be like once a specific goal is achieved, it can provide a motivating feeling of happiness and joy.

- **Keep your Eye on the Finish Line.**

  Understand that finishing what you start is important. Hammer into your mind that whatever you start you must finish. Develop the habit of going to the finish line.

- **Constantly Affirm your Success.**

  All affirmations are positive declarations, statements or judgments. Affirmations can be a powerful source of strength and focus. They can be repeated to yourself out loud or silently in your head to help affirm to yourself that you can, and will succeed.

How to Lead and Motivate Yourself?

AS LEADERS, WE KNOW that one of our major responsibilities is to keep our team motivated. To do so, we must constantly remind our people of the organization's vision, hold them accountable to targets and goals, mentor them and support them in their work. But, how does the one who motivates others every day stay motivated as well?

When it comes to leaders, motivation is really about engagement. How engaged are you in your work? How committed are you to the results you are supposed to be getting? Are you pushing forward with a sense of purpose and drive, or are you simply going through motions? To do your best and to obtain maximum Leadership Advantage, you need to give serious thought to what makes you flourish and succeed.

When you are motivated, you are a wholehearted participant in your own life. You know what is important to you and you use it as a guide. You feel confident, energized and engaged. However, when you are de-motivated, you *"lose your edge."* Your energy goes down. Your stress goes up. You may even feel guilty and resentful. You might even become bored and actually tune-out.

Whatever way a lack of motivation hits you, one thing is for sure – it is not a fun place to be. Whether you feel your motivation is waning or you want to keep your current high level of motivation on a roll, the following suggestions will help you stay at your best.

- **Stay Connected to What you are Doing.**

  It is one thing to do the work you are paid to do. It is another thing to be fulfilled by the work you do. If you are strictly doing your job for the money, or the title, or the company car, you could find that over time it is harder and harder to actually do the job.

  However, if you are connected to what you do and you are connected to what excites you, you will feel motivated to keep going because you will be achieving a bigger purpose for yourself.

The vital thing is to know your values. Your values are the principles, standards and qualities that guide you. To uncover your values, you may have to recall a time in your life when everything was "just right." You could choose something from your personal life or your work. You might revisit a moment, a particular event, or a whole phase of your life. Once you have allowed yourself some time to explore the memory, ask yourself what it was about that memory that made it so memorable, so significant, and so right. What made it a peak experience? Write down any ideas that come to mind – words, phrases, images and symbols. When you have finished with your notes, circle the words that meet the definition of values, including principles, standards and qualities. There is no right or wrong during this process. Simply use your own words and your gut to tell you what your values are.

¤ **Know What it Takes to Get Better.**

Motivation comes from constantly learning how to be better. Therefore, you should always be asking yourself, "What am I trying to achieve?" and "What do I need to learn to reach my goal?" You should realize that this is not about taking a workshop or reading a book. It is about challenging yourself to take on something new and to stretch yourself to a new level of results.

The fact is that when you practice learning as an element of motivational leadership, you too will stay motivated and you get better results for yourself, for your Associates and for your work. By learning, you empower yourself to have, do and be whatever you choose. And with empowerment comes confidence. You do not second-guess yourself or worry you will fail, because you know if you get it wrong, you will be able to figure out how to get it right.

- **Find the Right Support System.**

When you are a leader, all of the people below you must lean on you. You guide them, support them and tell them what to do.

However, when you are on top, you do not have anyone above you to lean on. That is when you need to look outside of your organization, your role or even your industry for the people who can cheer you on, mentor you and help you be your best. To do so, look for people whose style you like. They should be people who inspire you by the way they lead and the results they get. Seek out people who resonate with you and who seem to mirror parts of yourself. You should connect with them to see what is possible for you as a leader. You should learn how you can become more with the help of others who have already done what you want to do. The more carefully you build your support team, the more powerful it will be. You should not ask people to mentor you because you like them. You should make them a part of your team because they enhance you. The people on your support team can help you stay motivated. They can expand you by giving you access to what you do not know. Remember, it does not have to be lonely at the top.

- **Maintain a Sense of Balance.**

While maintaining work and life balance is not a way to stay motivated, it is a way to keep from becoming demotivated. When you are serving everyone else, you have to remember to fill your own tank. Remember that being an effective and motivated leader should not come at the expense of quality of life and your quality of life should not come at the expense of business results. Work and life should be able to co-exist, happily and successfully.

The key is to define what that balance looks like for you. If you are a senior leader, balance may not look very traditional. It might not be a nine-to-five job, Monday through Friday, with holidays and weekends off. You need to understand what works for you and what fulfills you in your personal life. What helps you restore your energy and find that sense of peace, rest and renewal? Depending on your lifestyle and personal preferences, that could be taking a morning job, sleeping in on days off, reading a fiction book or spending time with family.

The chart on the following page summarizes the personal goals you should pursue to enable *Motivation* to play a role in helping you maximize your *Leadership Advantage.*

Average Level of Motivation	Maximum Level of Motivation
You sometimes find yourself not connected to what you are doing and find it difficult to stay alert, focused and motivated.; or	You make sure you stay connected to what you're doing, it excites you and you feel motivated to keep going.
You are occasionally searching for what you need to do to get better and many times settle for mediocre performances; or	You know what it takes to get better and challenge yourself by stretching for better results.
You find yourself on the top and don't have anyone above you to lean on. You struggle to find the right support system; or	You seek out and connect with people who resonate with you to maintain peak levels of motivation.
You often feel like you are always serving everyone else and forget to fill your own tank; or	You maintain a good sense of work/life balance as a way to keep from becoming demotivated. *This is your Leadership Advantage*

CHAPTER EIGHT
LEADERSHIP AND UNSELFISHNESS

"A wise unselfishness is not a surrender of yourself to the wishes of anyone, but only to the best discoverable course of action."

— David Seabury
American psychologist, author, and lecturer

LEADERSHIP AND **UNSELFISHNESS**

WE ALL HAVE LEARNED that being an effective team member requires a degree of compromise and unselfishness. Well, it is even more important to understand the role that unselfishness and compromise play for us as leaders and in our ability to maximize our Leadership Advantage.

Unselfishness is a very popular ideal, one that has been honored throughout recorded history. Unselfishness is commonly defined as having or showing more concern for other people than for yourself; i.e. not being selfish. However, from an organizational and leadership perspective, my experience has taught me to think of unselfishness as much more than *"having or showing more concern for other people."* In terms of your Leadership Advantage, unselfishness is a key leadership trait that is both noticed and valued by others.

Professionally, a competent leader who is unselfish and who has the best interests of the organization at heart has followers who duly recognize this attribute. As such, they will offer a level of support that could provide significant advantage in difficult times. Personally, as you continue your quest to develop your skills and to become the best you, unselfishness will increase your chances by attracting and maintaining the strong support of others.

Now, my experience has taught me that unselfishness is not only essential to setting the foundation of a good leader but it is also a skill that must be developed. Your willingness and ability to sacrifice for others and put your own personal needs and desires second, requires focus.

It also requires sensitivity and understanding of another trait that is often misunderstood, which is compromise.

Webster's New World Dictionary defines compromise as primarily *"a settlement in which each side gives up some demands or makes concessions."* Unfortunately, the word compromise has become a judgmental term, something similar to selling out. In reality, compromise means working things out, or as Webster's says in a secondary meaning, *"an adjustment of opposing principles."*

As such, compromise is essential to getting things done, not only in your professional life but also in your personal and civil life. It can mean the difference between failure and success. Compromise is essential to any negotiations process.

As an Absolute Attribute, *Unselfishness* is anchored by compromise. An unselfish leader's openness and generosity is very likely to accrue significant benefits in both a personal and professional sense. A selfish leader who grabs all the credit and deflects all the blame will, at some point, find the world a very lonely place.

In this chapter we will first briefly explore three perspectives that you should embrace while leading yourself, your organization or your family through compromise. They are:

- ¤ Positive Intent Makes the Process of Compromise Productive;
- ¤ Collaboration is a Way to Achieve Effective Compromise; and
- ¤ Synergy is a Positive Result of Great Compromise.

Then, we will explore some examples which can help to answer two common questions that many experienced leaders ask themselves: *"What is it that unselfish leaders do and how do they behave?"*

Three Perspectives to use in Leading through Compromise

THE ART OF LEADING is not kicking the can down the road. Those who take full advantage of their Leadership Advantage pick the can up, understand its' contents and determine how, whatever is inside, can be resolved or refreshed to improve their personal or organizational performance as well as the lives of the people involved. Unselfishness and compromise are valuable tools in your arsenal.

Here are three perspectives that you should embrace while leading through compromise.

1. **Positive Intent makes the Process of Compromise Productive**

   If you go into a situation requiring compromise, then go into it with a positive attitude on how to bring people together and focus on developing a real, better solution. Others in the room will be different than you and will have different values and ideas on how to solve an issue. Listen positively. Engage with the intent to solve. Keep focused on the larger objective and what it requires.

2. **Collaboration is a Way to Achieve Effective Compromise**

   Collaboration is working together, leveraging another's strengths and finding ways to create a better solution. Ideas enhanced and supported by a larger group will gain strength and momentum. Adopt a collaborative mindset as you approach the problem, the challenge, the choice and the decision.

3. **Synergy is a Positive Result of Great Compromise**

   Rather than focusing on a minimal compromise or just continued disagreement, focus on synergy. Given the higher goal and the different ideas, how can they be brought together in the best way and create a better-than-incremental solution?

In other words, go beyond just compromise and create a better opportunity for success together.

What is it that Unselfish Leaders Do and How do they Behave?

The process of leading others is a human endeavor, not a science that can be quantified and categorized to fit into a neat set of instructions for success. Every individual is gifted with different levels of ability and capability to lead others. However, the resulting success or failure is not solely based on those abilities. Here are some examples of what many leaders do and how they behave when they successfully deploy an effective and meaningful degree of unselfishness and compromise.

- **Shares the Credit.**

Associates, who are recognized for their winning efforts, whether in the foreground or background, feel a sense of pride in and loyalty to their company and their leader. Since everyone wants to work for such a leader, a deep pool of talent very often ensues.

- **Takes the Time to Teach.**

Teaching is a critical role for a leader. The unselfish leader finds the time to teach Associates not only about business processes and results, company goals and objectives, but also about ethical, behavioral and civil standards that are important to the organization and the leader.

- **Accepts Responsibility for their Associates' Shortcomings.**

An unselfish leader is not quick to blame others or make excuses when Associates inevitably mess up. The leader first finds the fix to the problem, followed by coaching and counseling, and then looks for ways to improve the process and the training. Learning from mistakes is critical to continuous improvement. Giving Associates room to make mistakes and allow them to learn and gain confidence as a result, is an unselfish and courageous act for a leader.

- **Accepts and Shares the Ideas and Input of Others.**

An unselfish leader is open to new ideas and concepts, and from a variety of sources. So very often the Associates actually doing the work have the best ideas on how a particular process can be improved. Let others be the experts. Build the bench strength by developing technical and leadership skills in your Associates. Help others to succeed and reinforce the "unselfish" trait.

The chart on the next page summarizes the personal goals you should pursue to enable *Unselfishness* to play a role in helping you maximize your *Leadership Advantage.*

Average Level of Unselfishness	Maximum Level of Unselfishness
You feel that you can more than adequately respond to any situation that requires you to be less selfish and to compromise; or	You work on developing the skills to be unselfish and to compromise as required to achieve the best outcomes.
You approach most situations with the solution that you feel is best and a strategy to persuade the team; or	You approach all situations requiring compromise, with a positive attitude and focus on developing the best solution.
You only recognize Associates and others for outstanding effort and only to the degree to which they deserve recognition; or	You always recognize the efforts of Associates and others as well as ensure that they share in all rewards to the greatest extent possible.
You are usually as unselfish as you need to be and generally only compromise if it is the last resort; or	You know that unselfishness is anchored by compromise and you work to improve your skills in both areas. *This is your Leadership Advantage*

CHAPTER NINE
LEADERSHIP AND **DELIBERATION**

"Deliberation, n.: The act of examining one's bread to determine which side it is buttered on."

—Ambrose Bierce

American editorialist, journalist, short story writer

LEADERSHIP AND **DELIBERATION**

WE ALL HAVE "some" ability to be thoughtful and deliberate. But how can we prevent too much deliberation or the lack of deliberation from negatively impacting our ability to reach our goals. Well, in terms of maximizing your *Leadership Advantage*, deliberation is something that cannot be measured by too much or too little. Deliberation is a combination of a process and an art. In the broadest terms, leadership in itself is the art of leading others to deliberately create a result that wouldn't have happened otherwise.

The noun deliberation comes from the Latin word "deliberare", meaning "weigh," or "consider well." When you guide your team through all of the possible solutions to a problem, you are in deliberation. Deliberation is a carefully thought-out process of deciding, setting a course of action and following through with concise execution.

As one of the *Ten Absolute Attributes* associated with your Leadership Advantage, *Deliberation* is an artful process which delivers results and satisfaction as well as a sense of involvement.

When we deliberate with others, the deliberation process is collaborative and involves more than just one person's experience, needs and perspective. At its best, deliberation requires commitment on the part of all who enter into the process to listen to the perspectives and the knowledge of all who are participating and to try to learn from one another.

In this chapter we will explore the following aspects of the process of deliberation and how you, as a leader, can leverage this attribute to generate even better outcomes:

- How is Deliberation Different from Debate?
- Why is it Important to Know How to Deliberate?
- What are some Basic Guidelines for Deliberation? and
- What are some Tips for Facilitating the Deliberation Process?

How is Deliberation Different from Debate?

DELIBERATION IS NOT FOREIGN. In some way, it is very familiar to all of us. When we have to make an important decision, we deliberate. We consider the merits of a range of alternatives and weigh the advantages as well as the tradeoffs of each. After thinking the issue through, we try to make the best possible choice.

We then select the one that best addresses our particular needs. It may not be perfect, but it is informed by all of the information that we can bring to the decision at that time.

In a deliberation, everyone expects to end up in a different place as a result of the discussion and decisions made. You contribute your knowledge and perspective to the whole, listening to and building on the contributions of others. By engaging in shared ideas, everyone grows in knowledge, skills, insight, and understanding.

Deliberation is not a debate. In a debate, you hold onto your position with the intent that you will "win" the argument and everyone else will end up in a different place. Debate is a competitive process in which there are winners and losers. Ideas are not built. Ideas are contested. Deliberation is a more collaborative process.

The aim of deliberation is to share perspectives and knowledge and to build ideas; not to defend them.

Why is it Important to Know How to Deliberate?

AS PROFESSIONALS, we all know why debate skills are useful. We use these skills when we want to persuade another of the merits of our ideas. But what if our ideas are not fully formed? What if the issue is complex and involves multiple interests? How do you generate new approaches.

This calls for careful listening and being open to the knowledge and the views of others. It requires building new ideas and new approaches together. This is deliberation. Deliberation is a cornerstone of true leadership and for maximizing your Leadership Advantage. Professionally, learning and enhancing deliberative skills will increase your capacity to make better decisions, build stronger teams and develop the skills of your entire organization. In your personal and civic life, these skills and the mastery of the art will allow you to better connect with others and to form stronger relationships.

What are Some Basic Guidelines for Deliberation?

HERE ARE SEVEN BASIC GUIDELINES that can aid in maintaining a high level of consciousness when you engage in the deliberation process in almost any setting.

1. Always speak your mind freely, but do not monopolize the conversation. You should enter the deliberation with some knowledge of all the others that are involved and cognizant of the personalities and pressures.
2. Listen carefully to others. Do not fall into the trap of gathering your thoughts while someone else is speaking. You may miss some the key points that are being made, but you should try to really understand what others are saying and respond to them fully. This is especially important when their ideas are different from your own.
3. You should avoid building your own argument in your head while others are talking. If you are afraid you will forget a point, write it down.

4. Paraphrase the points of view of others to help confirm the understanding of their points and positions.
5. Be open to changing your mind. This will help you really listen to others' points of view.
6. When disagreement occurs, do not personalize it. Keep talking and explore the disagreement. Look for the common concerns beneath the surface.
7. Be careful not to discredit another person's point of view. Remember that, although you are trying to listen to and build on each other's ideas, remember, it does not mean that everyone has to end up in the same place.

What are some Tips for Facilitating the Deliberation Process?

AS A LEADER TASKED WITH the facilitation of a deliberative session, you are responsible for maintaining the flow of the discussion, encouraging opportunities for participation, and assuring a respectful and open environment that allows for the meaningful discussion and exchange of views that take place in a successful deliberative process. Here are some proven tips that will aid in both facilitating the deliberation process as well as leveraging some inherited leadership skills.

- Listen actively.
- Engage everyone in the discussion.
- Do not speak after each comment or answer every question.
- Encourage participants to talk to each other, not to you.
- Help the group to look at the issues from many different points of view.
- If one or more perspectives are not getting a fair hearing, ask if someone in the group can make a case for that view.

¤ Help the group to identify and summarize commonality as the discussion move forward. However, you should not force it.

The following chart summarizes the personal goals you should pursue to enable *Deliberation* to play a role in helping you maximize your *Leadership Advantage.*

Average Level of Deliberation	Maximum Level of Deliberation
You enter deliberation only when you are not able to sell your idea or position outright without getting others involved; or	**You see deliberation as a process which can aid in making the best possible choice.**
You prepare for a deliberation as you would a debate or any competitive process in which there are winners and losers; or	**You consider a strategic range of alternatives and weigh the advantages as well as the tradeoffs of each when you deliberate.**
You strategically guard your thoughts and points-of-view until the best time to score points and move the discussion in your favor; or	**You always speak your mind freely, but don't monopolize the conversation while in deliberation sessions.**
You understand that the aim of deliberation is to share and listen to other perspectives but find it a waste of time when you feel that you have the right answer; or	**You know that the aim of deliberation is to share perspectives and to build ideas, not to defend them.** ***This is your Leadership Advantage***

"Success is not final; failure is not fatal: it is the courage to continue that counts."

— Winston S. Churchill
British statesman

CHAPTER TEN
LEADERSHIP AND **COURAGE**

"Courage is the most important of all the virtues because without courage, you can't practice any other virtue consistently."

— Maya Angelou
American poet, memoirist, actress

LEADERSHIP AND **COURAGE**

WE ALL HAVE some mental or moral strength to persevere and withstand danger, fear, or difficulty. However, because courage is required in almost every basic human activity or endeavor, how do we ration our courageousness consistent with results that can be expected?

Certainly, courage in our daily lives can sometimes be a matter of life and death. In some occupations like being a police officer or firefighter you are expected to routinely take courageous actions. The courage in these occupations seems to be instinctive and reactionary. However, there have been many studies on human behavior in organizations and they all seem to indicate that courage in business seldom operates like this. Leaders who act courageously, whether on behalf of society, their companies, their colleagues or their own career rarely do it impulsively. Nor does it emerge from nowhere.

In business, courageous action is really a special kind of calculated risk taking. As we discussed in the previous chapter, those of us who become good leaders have a greater than average willingness to make bold moves, but they strengthen their chances of success, and avoid career suicide, through careful deliberation and preparation.

Business courage is not so much a visionary leader's inborn characteristic as it is a skill acquired through decision-making processes that improve with practice. In other words, to maximize your Leadership Advantage you must teach yourself how to make high-risk decisions. Much of the ability to be a truly courageous leader is learned and leverages the skills associated with the other nine *Absolute Attributes.* You should always remember courageous leadership blossoms over time.

As Mark Twain once wrote, *"Courage is not the absence of fear, but its mastery."* Mastering the concept of courageous leadership and taking intelligent risks requires an understanding of what I call *"Calculated Risk and Reward."*

Calculated Risk and Reward is a straight-forward approach of making leadership success more likely while avoiding impulsive, unproductive or irrational behavior. In business, as in life, taking positive, calculated risks is sometimes absolutely necessary in order to achieve an elusive goal or the next level of performance. As with any risk, there is always something at stake. In most instances, when it comes to leadership decisions, you stand to lose money, time, respect and your reputation. Which are also the very same things you stand to gain. The rewards of having an appropriate level of disciplined courage and taking risks can enrich your business, your career and your life.

In this chapter we will briefly discuss the following six discrete steps that make up the *Calculated Risk and Reward* approach to taking courageous leadership actions.

- Setting Primary and Secondary Goals
- Determining the Importance of Achieving Your Goals
- Tipping the Power Balance in Your Favor
- Weighing Risks against Rewards
- Selecting the Proper Time for Action
- Developing Contingency Plans

1. Setting Primary and Secondary Goals

The first step of the Calculated Risk and Reward approach is for you to answer these questions:

- What will success look like? Is it realistically obtainable?

- If my primary goal is organizational, does it defend or advance my company's or team's principles and values?
- If my primary goal is personal, does it derive solely from my career ambitions or also from a desire for my organization's or even society's greater good?
- If I cannot meet my primary goal, what is my secondary goal?

Whether primary or secondary, your goals should be reasonably within reach and not pie-in-the-sky ambitions.

A primary goal that serves the organization might be either to rescue a good Associate or to prevent the senior manager from acting on defective information. A secondary organizational goal might be to apprise a senior manager of internal "people challenges" that are hidden deep in the organization.

A primary goal that serves you personally might be to receive some behind-the-scenes credit for helping the Associate. A secondary personal goal might be to feel that you did something for the greater good.

2. Determining the Importance of Achieving Your Goals

The second step of the Calculated Risk and Reward approach addresses these questions:

- Just how important is it that you achieve your goal or goals?
- If you do not do something about the current state of affairs, will your organization suffer?
- Will your career be derailed?
- Will you be able to look at yourself in the mirror? Does the situation call for immediate, high-profile action or something more nuanced and less risky?

Remember, courageous leadership is not about wasting political capital on low-priority issues.

To distinguish such squandering from constructive risk, you should assign importance to three levels. On the *lowest rung* are issues about which you do not feel strongly, though you may prefer a particular outcome and may address in a low-risk situation. *Middle-rung* issues are those about which your opinion is strong but does not involve higher values. That is, your feelings may change based on new information. At the *top of the ladder* are "fight-worthy" issues. Fight-worthy issues are those that rest on morals or values for which you are willing to take a stand and fight.

3. Tipping the Power Balance in Your Favor

Sometimes, even as seasoned professionals, we often assume that power in our organization is a simple matter of position on the organization chart. In attempting to please more senior leaders, we may choose never to take a stand. But in reality, even those in top management give power to anyone on whom they are dependent—whether for respect, advice, friendship, appreciation or network affiliations.

Seen this way, organizational power is something over which we really do have considerable control. By establishing relationships with and influencing those around you, for example, you gain sway over people who otherwise hold sway over you. This gives you a broader base from which to make bold moves.

4. Weighing Risks Against Rewards

This step of the Calculated Risk and Reward approach focuses on trade-offs and can present these questions:

- Who stands to win?
- Who stands to lose?
- What are the chances that your reputation will be tarnished beyond repair if you go forward?
- Will you lose respect or your job? or cause others to lose theirs?
- Delay your opportunity for promotion?

Other trade-offs deal with the quality of the action and the strategy involved. Are your goals better served if you act in a direct and forceful way or if you take an indirect approach?

5. Selecting the Proper Time for Action

Desmond Tutu, the South African social rights activist and former Anglican bishop, once described great leaders as having an uncanny sense of timing. *"The real leader,"* he writes, knows *"when to make concessions, when to compromise, when to employ the art of losing the battle in order to win the war."*

It can be argued that when someone is confronted by a situation that requires courage, the question of timing should be irrelevant. Being in leadership roles sometimes move us to assume that in "fight-worthy" situations, when much is at stake and emotions are running high, brave people do not hesitate to act. This may be true in emergency situations, but a single-minded rush to action in business is usually foolish.

Although emotion is always in the mix, and may even be an asset when making a courageous leadership move, the following questions can help in logically calculating whether the time is right:

- Why am I pursuing this now?
- Am I contemplating a considered action or an impulsive one?
- How long would it take to become better prepared? Is that too long?
- What are the pros and cons of waiting a day, two days, a week or more?
- What are the political obstacles? Can these be either removed or reduced in the near future?
- Can I take steps now that will create a foundation for a courageous move later?
- Am I emotionally and mentally prepared to take this risk?

- Do I have the expertise, communication skills, track record, and credibility to make this work?

Spending too much time on any or all of these questions, of course, can lead you into Hamlet's trap, and the opportunity for courage may pass you by.

At the same time, too little consideration may result in an overly hasty leap. It is important to remember that courageous action in business is for the most part deliberative. Real emergencies are rare. Time may well be on your side. Before you make your move, it is critical to marshal sufficient support, information or evidence to improve your odds of success.

6. Developing Contingency Plans

In general, contingency planning is about resourcefulness. Leaders who take bold risks and succeed are versatile thinkers; they ready themselves with alternative routes. Courageous leaders prepare themselves for any eventuality, including worst-case scenarios.

In the end, courage in business, as in life, rests on priorities that serve a personal, an organizational, or a societal philosophy. When this philosophy is bolstered by clear, obtainable primary and secondary goals; an evaluation of their importance; a favorable power base; a careful assessment of risks versus benefits; appropriate timing; and well-developed contingency plans; you are better empowered to make bold moves that serve your organization, your career and your own sense of personal worth.

The following chart summarizes the personal goals you should pursue to enable *Courage* to play a role in helping you maximize your *Leadership Advantage.*

Average Level of Courage	Maximum Level of Courage
You think through each issue which requires risky leadership actions, but do not take the time to consider both primary and secondary options; or	You always set primary and secondary goals in your approach to taking potentially risky leadership actions.
You usually sense situations which require strong leadership action, react accordingly and hope the action is appropriate; or	You always determine if the situation calls for immediate, high-profile action or something more nuanced and less risky.
You sometimes consider available trade-offs before taking risky leadership actions but normally depend on your "gut-feelings;" or	You always weigh risks against rewards and consider available trade-offs before taking risky leadership actions.
You tend to act quickly and take risky actions without considering the timeliness when emotions are in the mix; or	You value the need for an uncanny sense of timing when making a courageous leadership move. *This is your Leadership Advantage*

CHAPTER ELEVEN
LEADERSHIP AND **RESPECT**

LEADERSHIP AND **RESPECT**

WE ALL DESIRE TO BE RESPECTED and we understand its value in getting things done through others. But, are we capable of consistently giving the proper level of respect to situations and circumstances as well as to individuals?

The 21st century workplace continue to evolve, and for the most part, has become more trustworthy, transparent, ethical, collaborative and mindful of its team members.

Today's leaders must be equally diligent to earn respect from their Associates and their colleagues. Being the leader does not mean that you have earned respect. Too many of us take our titles and authority for granted. Some of us believe that we are owed or command some level of respect just because of where we are positioned on the organizational chart. Today's workplace is highly influenced by millennials and embedded with people that have trouble trusting others, in general. They require proof of performance before respect is earned. Thus, as 21st century leaders, we must reset our state of mind and become more responsible with our actions and accountable for the effect our influence has on our teams and the organization as a whole.

As one of the Ten *Absolute Attribute*s associated with maximizing your Leadership Advantage, *Respect* is more than just a word. The context of this attribute challenges us to consider what it truly means and what it distinguishes for us. This can make a significant difference in how we observe ourselves, others and our organization. Conventional wisdom considers "respect" to be a kind of feeling or a judgment of a person's "worthiness". However, respect can also be a declaration on the part of the person who is respecting another. If we take this to be the case, then respect is something else altogether.

In this chapter, we will explore the following aspects of Leadership and Respect;

- What is Respect?
- What is Respectful Leadership? and
- How to Leverage the Five Fundamental Pillars of Leadership to Earn Respect of your Team?

What is Respect?

RESPECT IS ONE OF THE VALUES that have been talked about a lot in organizations. Respect is a word that always evokes a positive conversation. The challenge has been that most leaders rarely think about or understand what it means to respect someone, to create a culture of respect among people or, for that matter, what it means to be respected. Most of us believe that respect is an important value and that it is good. We do not normally think of respect as an action but as a feeling or judgment about other people.

Whether respect is declared or whether it occurs as a judgment, it is an expression of the way the person who is respecting, or not respecting, sees themselves and others. Respect is in the eye of the beholder and is not a function of the behaviors or the attributes of those with whom we are interacting.

Furthermore, many of us propose that to understand respect as an empowering concept, it must also be universal. If respect is a judgment, it becomes a tool of the ego and actually a source of separation and conflict between human beings. The alternative is to understand that respect is an action, a declaration and a commitment on our part of who another person *is* --- separate and apart from whatever judgments we might have of his or her behavior. If we say we respect someone, we are "looking" at the other person in a particular way — usually suggesting we are open to listen and honor each other's views even if we disagree. If we say we do not respect someone, we are generally "closed" to certain opportunities, possibilities, and conversations with them.

Likewise, if we have "self-respect" we are generally in a healthy internal conversation with ourselves. If we do not respect ourselves, we will typically be stuck in all sorts of unproductive and unsatisfying "self-talk". If we say that something is possible to someone we respect, we will more than likely have a productive and satisfying dialogue. If we do not respect them then we will more than likely be closed, not listen or in some cases disregard and dismiss them and their views outright.

What is Respectful Leadership?

The term, *Respectful Leadership* is a complex one. It has a variety of meanings depending on the context in which it is used. However, respected leaders are most often defined as leaders who consult with their subordinates, respect their expertise and their value to the organization. Respected leaders seem to be able to deternine how they want to be treated and what they consider is respectful to them. They send out a powerful message that actively encourages both self-respect as well as respect for others.

Here are some suggestions that could help you move in the direction of being viewed as a respectful leader.

- **Take a Top Down Approach.**

  Most good leaders encourage Associates to respect both themselves and others. However, many of these leaders often fail to perceive that respect starts at the top. The way to create a more respectful workplace is to make respect a centerpiece of your leadership approach.

- **Encourage Civility.**

  Bad manners and questionable behavior should not be viewed as acceptable in any professional workplace. Respectful leadership promotes workplace civility and prepares Associates with conflict resolution skills and processes.

- **Emphasize Communication.**

  Respectful leaders are great communicators. One of the keys to creating an atmosphere of respect in any business or organization is to include your Associates in your decision-making processes to the fullest extent possible. Although it should always be clear that you are the final decision maker, you will gain the respect of your team if you listen to their input and communicate the rationale behind your decisions.

- **Create Partnerships with Team Members.**

  Inclusion and collaboration are critical features of respectful leadership. If you treat your team members simply as Associates, you will never gain their full respect. However, if you treat them like valuable partners in executing your organization's mission, they will reward you with their trust, loyalty, and respect.

- **Recognize Employee Contributions.**

  It is difficult to respect a leader that takes all of the credit for organizational successes. Respectful leaders recognize the contributions their team members make to their success.

Five Fundamental Pillars of Leadership to Earn the Respect of your Team

TO HELP YOU ACHIEVE sustainable success as a leader who puts people first, here are five ways to earn the respect of your team.

1. Maintain Consistently Strong Work Ethic and Set Standards

Actions are stronger than words, and this is personified by the respected leader. Great leaders rebuff false promises and people that create lots of unnecessary noise to get attention. There are many leaders that play the role on the outside, but have very little substance on the inside. Respected leaders are those who consistently prove through their work ethic that they are reliable and trustworthy on the inside and out.

These leaders set the tone and are great role models. The tangible and measurable results of their consistent work ethic influence new best practices and cultivate innovation. Ultimately, their leadership defines the performance culture for the organization. They set the standard and leave behind a permanent impact.

2. Do Not be Afraid to Take Risks and Admit it When You are Wrong

Respected leaders are those who are not afraid to take risks. They are bold enough to change the conversation and seamlessly challenge the status quo for the betterment of the organization and their competitive advantage. They can anticipate when a paradigm shift is in order and are courageous enough to act on it.

The other side of this admirable trait is the ability to admit wrong doing. Respected leaders do not hesitate to make the most difficult decisions and will put themselves out on the frontline to lead by example. When it is appropriate, they gravitate towards what many view as a "leap of faith" and willingly accept the challenge – knowing very well that the odds may not be in their favor given the personalities and inherent obstacles that surround them.

3. Sponsor High-Potential Associates

Respected leaders think about making others better. They are mindful of those that give one hundred percent of themselves toward their responsibilities. Respected leaders find ways to discover the best in people and enable their full potential. When they detect high-potential talent they impart upon them their wisdom and provide a path for long-term success.

Leaders that "sponsor" their Associates put their own reputation at risk for the betterment of the individuals they are serving. This is an admirable quality and one that is highly respected among a leader's peers.

4. Present a Powerful Executive Presence

As I mentioned in the earlier chapters, the most respected leaders are the most authentic people. Their executive presence is genuine and true. They make those around them feel that they matter and they welcome constructive dialogue regardless of hierarchy or rank.

Respected leaders trust themselves enough to live their personal brand and serve as powerful role models to others. Their presence create a long-lasting impact that leaves a positive mark on the organization and the people they serve. Respected leaders are passionate, impact-driven people. Their presence is felt when they walk into the room. Their reputation and their track record precede them.

5. Give Credit to your Team and Reward Performance

Too many leaders are recognition addicts and want all of the credit. They spend too much time breaking down rather than building up their teams. They do not take the time to genuinely learn about other's needs. Leadership is ultimately about knowing the people you serve and giving them the guidance, inspiration and navigational tools to make their lives better and enable more opportunities.

Leaders earn respect when they reward and recognize their Associates and colleagues. They take the time to appreciate and understand the unique ways they each think, act and innovate; and are always on the lookout to enable their talent. They are trusted, admired and respected because they make it more about the advancement of others, rather than themselves. They share the harvest of the momentum they build with others.

Earning respect is a journey and requires leaders to focus on how they can "deliver beyond what is expected" of their role and responsibilities. It is about always being on the look-out for ways to improve and being mindful of ways to make the workplace better and the organization and its people more competitive and relevant.

The chart on the next page summarizes the personal goals you should pursue to enable *Respect* to play a role in helping you maximize your *Leadership Advantage.*

Average Level of Respect	Maximum Level of Respect
You feel that you naturally respect others, but you never challenge the congruency of your view of respect and your leadership style; or	You believe that respect is an important value and that this view helps to create a culture of respect within your team and the entire organization.
You normally think of respect as a feeling and a judgment about other people, even though you know this view can create a source of separation and conflict; or	You understand that respect is a determination, on your part, of "who another person is" and should be separate from judgments you might have regarding their behavior.
You believe that you are owed some level of respect just because of where you are positioned on the organizational chart; or	You know that you are not owed a level of respect simply because of your leadership role. You work to gain the respect of others.
You work hard at maintaining an acceptable "work brand" that is separate from your personal brand.; or	You know that the most respected leaders are the most authentic people. *This is your Leadership Advantage*

"Respect yourself and others will respect you."

— Confucius
Chinese teacher, editor, politician, and philosopher

CHAPTER TWELVE
LEADERSHIP AND **FOCUS**

LEADERSHIP AND **FOCUS**

WE ALL HAVE some ability to direct our attention to events and activities when it is apparent that there is a need or a problem. However, do we have natural instinct or sufficient skill to ensure that the proper focus is always where it needs to be?

As we all know, becoming an effective leader is not a one-time thing. It takes time to learn and practice all of the required leadership skills. However, according to psychologist Daniel Coleman, *"staying focused turns out to be one of the most important leadership skills"*

In terms of leadership, when we speak about being focused, we commonly mean thinking about one thing while filtering out distractions. But a wealth of recent research in neuroscience shows that effective leaders focus in many ways, for different purposes, drawing on different neural pathways. Some paths seem to work in concert, while others tend to stand in opposition.

One way to shed new light on the practice of this essential leadership attribute is by grouping the *modes* of focus into the following three areas:

- Focusing on Yourself;
- Focusing on Others; and
- Focusing on the Wider World.

Focusing inward and focusing constructively on others helps us, as leaders, cultivate the primary elements of emotional intelligence. A deeper and broader understanding of how we focus on the *wider world* can improve our ability to develop strategy, innovate, and manage organizations.

In order to realize our maximum Leadership Advantage, we should cultivate this *triad of awareness*, in abundance and in the proper balance. Based on my experience, a failure to focus inward can leave you rudderless; a failure to focus on others can render you clueless at times; and a failure to focus outward may leave you blindsided.

In this chapter we will briefly explore these three *modes of focus* to help you understand how they work independently and how they work together.

Focusing on Yourself

AS MOST OF US ARE AWARE, emotional intelligence begins with self-awareness and getting in touch with our inner voice. Leaders who heed their inner voices can draw on more resources to make better decisions and connect with their authentic selves.

Hearing your inner voice is a matter of paying careful attention to internal physiological signals. These subtle cues are monitored by the *insula*, which is tucked behind the frontal lobes of the brain.

Attention given to any part of the body amps up the insula's sensitivity to that part. Tune in to your heartbeat, and the insula activates more neurons in that circuitry. How well people can sense their heartbeats has, in fact, become a standard way to measure their self-awareness.

Gut feelings are messages from the insula and the *amygdala*, which the neuroscientist Antonio Damasio, of the University of Southern California, calls "somatic markers." Those messages are sensations that something "feels" right or wrong. Somatic markers simplify decision making by guiding our attention toward better options.

To be authentic is to be the same person to others as you are to yourself. In part, that entails paying attention to what others think of you, particularly people whose opinions you esteem and who will be candid in their feedback. A variety of focus that is useful here is *open awareness*, in which we broadly notice what is going on around us without getting caught up in or swept away by any particular thing. In this mode we do not judge, censor, or tune out. We simply perceive.

Leaders who are more accustomed to giving input than to receiving it may find this difficult. Someone who has trouble sustaining *open awareness* typically gets snagged by irritating details. Of course, being open to input does not guarantee that someone will provide it. Sadly, life affords us few chances to learn how others really see us and even fewer for leaders as they rise through the ranks.

Focusing on Others

THE WORD "ATTENTION" comes from the Latin "attendere", meaning "to reach toward." This is a perfect definition of *focus on others*, which is the foundation of empathy and of an ability to build social relationships—the second and third pillars of emotional intelligence.

Leaders who can effectively focus on others are easy to recognize. They are the ones who find common ground, whose opinions carry the most weight and with whom other people want to work. They emerge as natural leaders regardless of organizational or social rank.

Having empathy, as a leader, is vital to your ability to focus on others. In order to appreciate the role empathy plays in leadership, we first need to have a clear understanding of what empathy means. Most times, we tend to confuse empathy with sympathy. We tend to believe that to be empathetic means agreeing or relating to the feelings another person has regarding a given situation or individual.

However, what empathy really means is being able to understand the needs of others. It means that you are aware of their feelings and how it impacts their perception. It does not mean you have to agree with how they see things. On the contrary, being empathetic means that you are willing and able to appreciate what the other person is going through.

We talk about empathy most commonly as a single attribute. But a close look at where leaders are focusing when they exhibit empathy reveals three distinct types. Each type is important to maximizing your Leadership Advantage.

Here is a brief explanation of the three categories.

The first type is called *Cognitive Empathy.* Cognitive empathy is the ability to understand another person's perspective. Cognitive empathy enables you to explain yourself in meaningful ways—a skill essential to getting the best performance from your direct reports. Contrary to what many might expect, exercising cognitive empathy requires you to think about feelings rather than to feel them directly.

The second type is called *Emotional Empathy.* Emotional empathy is the ability to feel what someone else feels. Emotional empathy is important for effective mentoring, managing clients and reading group dynamics. According to experts in the field, *"emotional empathy springs from ancient parts of the brain beneath the cortex—the amygdala, the hypothalamus, the hippocampus, and the orbitofrontal cortex—that allow us to feel fast without thinking deeply."* These parts of the brain seem to "tune us in" by arousing in our bodies the emotional states of others. It is widely believed that emotional empathy can be developed.

The third type is called *Empathic Concern.* Empathic concern is the ability to sense what another person needs from you. Empathic concern, which is closely related to emotional empathy, enables us to sense not just how people feel but what they need from you.

Focusing on the Wider World

LEADERS WITH A STRONG outward focus are not only good listeners but also good questioners. They are visionaries who can sense the far-flung consequences of local decisions and imagine how the choices they make today will play out in the future. They are open to the surprising ways in which seemingly unrelated data can inform their central interests.

Getting Them All to Work Together

CERTAINLY, AS A LEADER you do not want to end up similarly compartmentalized. So, getting all three *modes of focus* to work together is the key to being a truly focused leader.

You should not just focus on being the leader known for concentrating on the three most important priorities of the year, or the most brilliant systems thinker, or the one most in tune with the corporate culture. You must be able to command the full range of your own attention:

- You are in touch with your inner feelings;
- You can control your impulses;
- You are aware of how others see you;
- You understand what others need from you; and
- You can weed out distractions and also allow your mind to roam widely, free of preconceptions.

That is when you realize your maximum level of Leadership Advantage.

The chart on the next page summarizes the personal goals you should pursue to enable *Focus* to play a role in helping you maximize your *Leadership Advantage.*

Average Level of Focus	Maximum Level of Focus
You consider yourself focused when you think about one thing and just filter out distractions. ; or	You know that staying focused is one of your most important leadership skills and that your focus naturally spans a number of pathways.
You focus primarily on yourself and what you need to achieve. You consider others only when it is beneficial; or	You know that focusing inwardly as well as on others can help you cultivate the primary elements of emotional intelligence.
You hear your inner voice frequently but ignore it most of the time; or	You know that hearing your inner voice is a matter of paying careful attention to internal physiological signals.
You believe that being empathetic means agreeing with the feelings of others and that empathy has no place in your role as a leader; or	You utilize your empathy as a leader to enhance your constructive focus on others. *This is your Leadership Advantage*

EPILOGUE

LONG LIVE THE KING

THE PHRASES, *"The king is dead" and "long live the king,"* were first recorded in 1422 when Charles VI of France died, and his son Charles VII became king. It signifies the transition of power when a king dies, and it emphasizes that the kingdom remains intact despite the death of the current monarch. More on *"Long Live the King,"* a little later in this short essay.

But for now, I must admit that while reviewing the final draft of the manuscript of *"Becoming a Transformational Leader in the Post-Biden Era,"* and preparing the initial draft of this Epilogue, I thought it would be a good idea for me to write down the three main "takeaways" from this book, if I was a first-time reader.

Well. Here are my *three* takeaways.

My first takeaway. From my perspective, the picture being painted regarding the state of America's social and political affairs is fairly accurate. Especially when it is "read as written" and I can suppress my personal biases and preferred interpretations.

My second takeaway. Being a logical person, I would consider the thoughts presented to build the case for *Transformational Leaders* to naturally integrate the LV3 communications strategy into their daily work is novel and certainly passes the commonsense test.

The LV3 strategy, as presented, does appear to be structured as an effective "counter" to what the book tactfully characterizes as the *"psychological pickling,"* of partisans, which seems to have expanded the number of Americans seeking *change at any cost.*

The professional roles, unique abilities, and special skills of effective *Transformational Leaders*, along with the cast of people they must build trustful relationships with, puts them in the position to be successful at *transforming* more Americans to think more critically as well as to value the idea of *common good* in a broader context; and

My third takeaway. As candidly shared within the pages of the book, I have personally lived long enough to witness our country's democratic style of government, and the U.S. Constitution slowly move forward and adjust to the realities of life in the 21st century.

However, based on the unexpected and unprincipled dismantling of 80 years of struggle and hard work to build our national institutions, to improve our social fabric, and to earn our international standing in the world, I firmly believe that something must be done to halt and prevent this "pivot" into authoritarianism. I personally believe that it will be up to the American people to critically educate themselves regarding the *dangers* of choosing *popularity*, *partisanship*, *selfishness*, and/or *single-issue voting* over the undesirable *realities,* associated with damaging our *fragile* and *vulnerable* form of democracy.

Now, back to the phrase, "*The king is dead, long live the king*" and my response to a question that we all should be asking as we reflect to our nation's founding and seriously consider what's happening *politically* and *socially*, within the United States today.

This question is: *Why is this phrase so pertinent to how Americans should perceive and address the advent of the current "pivot" in federal governance based on our country's history as compared to what we are experiencing today?*

Now, with only five months into this politically motivated and financed "pivot" toward autocratic governance, here is my best three-point response to this question.

1. First and foremost, the United States has never been a Kingdom. Our country was founded on the principle of republicanism and the fight-worthy rejection of the *monarchy* of Great Britain. History states that *"some individuals considered George Washington as a potential king after the Revolutionary War, this idea was ultimately rejected, and the United States was established as a republic."*

   A strong rejection of any form of *monarchy*, should be a *"no brainer,"* which should instantly galvanize more than a plurality of Americans against the idea of having to choose between *"my politics"* or *"my democracy"*... *but nothing like what we are experiencing today.*

2. The *second point* is that accompanying this phrase back in the 15th century was a common understanding, by those within the kingdom, that the death of a king was not the end of the monarchy. It only *"signified the transition of power."*

   To date, America has had 60 Presidential inaugurations to *signify* the peaceful *transition of power* from one Federal Administration to the next. All the *transitions* have resulted in changes that have pushed our nation and our democracy forward and helped to create a stronger union... but *nothing like what we are experiencing today.*

3. The *third point* is that the phrase, *"The king is dead,"* used during that period was intended to clearly *"emphasize to the people that their kingdom [or their monarchy] remains <u>intact</u> despite the death of the current monarch."*

   Over the past 230 years, the changing of the *guards in our country*, be it a new president and a new congress, has been viewed as a trusted process. We all went to bed on election night, regardless of our political leaning, feeling safe and with *no worries* that "our kingdom" [*or our republic*] would not "remain intact" ...*but nothing like what we are experiencing today.*

Regardless of your political or social leaning, I feel that with your first read of *"Becoming a Transformational Leader in the Post-Biden Era,"* you will find throughout the book, a sincere attempt to be impartial and nonpartisan in the research and the presentation of the *facts,* and the *cultural reality,* that frame our country's current social and political dilemma.

Depending on your working knowledge and familiarity with the discipline of *Transformational Leadership* or the important roles of *Transformational Leaders*, I believe you will find the thought-provoking history and narratives on *leadership styles* and *traits*, the life-changing potential of the LV3 communications strategy, and the insightful leadership primer, somewhat captivating.

However, what you might miss during the first reading and pick up in subsequent readings and the discussion of the book with others, is the subtle and embedded references to America's **KING**.

This **KING** is the acronym for a combination of *leadership traits* that most Americans understand is mandatory for our country to continue to be democratically governed by *"We the People."*

It's the combination of our **K**nowledge, our **I**ndependence, our **N**imbleness, and our **G**ratitude, which has kept our democracy strong through a civil war, two world wars and multiple military, economic and social battles. However, it is the same **KING** that has shepherded the good and the bad in such a determined fashion that, America, in only a couple of centuries, has become the world standard for economic dominance, technological innovation, military power and cultural diversity.

Long Live the **KING**.

ABOUT THE AUTHOR

Ervin (Earl) Cobb is an accomplished corporate executive, leadership development coach, lecturer, and author.

He has held senior technical and leadership positions within Fortune 100, Mid-market and Venture companies including *Honeywell, Inc.*, *Motorola, Inc.*, *The Reynolds and Reynolds Company* and *Wells Fargo Bank*. He is the former President, COO and CEO of the high-tech start-up, *MedContrax, Inc.*

Earl earned a Bachelor of Science degree in Electrical Engineering, with honors, from *Tennessee State University*. He graduated from *Arizona State University* with a Master of Science degree in Engineering.

He is a former Adjunct Professor of Management at the Keller Graduate School of Management of *DeVry University*. He has completed graduate studies at *Stanford University's Graduate School of Business, the Sloan School of Management at MIT* and the *Center for Creative Leadership.*

Earl is the author of 17 published books and over 100 published articles.

REFERENCES

REFERENCES

1. Bass, B. M. (1985), *Leadership and Performance beyond Expectations.* Free Press, New York.
2. Bass, B. M. (1990), *From transactional to transformational leadership: Learning to share the vision. Organizational Dynamics 18,* 19-31.
3. Bass, B. M. and Avolio, B. J. (1989), *Manual for the Multifactor Leadership Questionnaire,* Consulting Psychologists Press, Palo Alto.
4. Bass, B. M. and Avolio, B. J. (1994) *Improving Organizational Effectiveness through Transformational Leadership,* Sage Publications, Thousand Oaks, CA.
5. Bass, B. M., Avolio, B. J., & Atwater, L. (1996). *The transformational and transactional leadership of men and women.* Applied Psychology: *An International Review, 45*, 5–34.
6. Bass, B. M., & Riggio, R. E. (2006), *Transformational leadership,*
7. Burns, J. M. (1978). *Leadership,* NY: Harper & Row.
8. Bass, B. M. (1999), *Two decades of research and development in transformational leadership. European journal of work and organizational psychology*, 8(1), 9-32.
9. Bass, B. M., & Avolio, B. J. (1993), *Transformational leadership and organizational culture.* Public administration quarterly, 112-121.
10. Bass, B. M., & Steidlmeier, P. (1999), *Ethics, character, and authentic transformational leadership behavior.* The leadership quarterly, 10(2), 181-217.

11. Bysystems (January 1, 2023), *How Politics Influence Our Daily Lives: A Closer Look,* Dan Emmett.

12. Chang, Jonathan and Chakrabarti, (August 2024), *How the Culture Wars Poisoned American Politics — and How to Fix It,* On Point.

13. Cobb, Ervin (2011) *Focus Leadership: What You Can Do Today to Become a More Effective Leader,* RICHER Press.

14. Cobb, Ervin (2015) *The Leadership Advantage: Do More ,Lead More. Earn More,* RICHER Press.

15. Cobb, Ervin (2024) *The Conscious Citizen: The Tough Questions The Average American Should Be Asking,* RICHER Press.

16. Cobb, Ervin (2011) Pillow *Talk Consciousness: Intimate Reflections on America's 100 Most Interesting Thoughts and Suspicions*, RICHER Press.

17. Cobb, Ervin and Grant-Cobb, Charlotte D. (2021) *Why Is It So Hard: Becoming A People Person in the Post COVID-19 Era,* RICHER Press.

18. Downton, J. V. (1973), *Rebel leadership: Commitment and charisma in a revolutionary process,* New York. Free Press.

19. Elliott Davis Jr. (2023*), Poll: Americans Are Down on Society's Leaders – Especially in Politics,* U.S. News & World Report.

20. Facing History & Ourselves (August 26, 2024), *"Political Polarization in the United States"*, Facinghistory.org.

21. Freud, Sigmund (2021), *Psychopathology of Everyday Life,* Fingerprint! Publishing.

22. Freud, Sigmund (1990) *The Ego and the Id (The Standard Edition of the Complete Psychological Works of Sigmund Freud),* W. W. Norton & Company.

23. Journal of Personality and Social Psychology: *The Political is Personal: The Costs of Daily Politics,* by Brett Q. Ford, PhD, Matthew Feinberg, PhD, and Bethany Lassetter, PhD, and Arasteh Gatchpazian, University of Toronto, and Sabrina Thai, PhD, Brock University. Jan. 23, 2023.

22. Maxwell Leadership (September 13, 2022), *10 Characteristics of a Growth Environment.*

23. Kahneman, Danzel. (2011), *Thinking, Fast and Slow*: Farrar, Straus and Giroux.

24. Kahneman, Daniel. (2022) *Noise: A Flaw in Human Judgment*, Little, Brown and Company.

25. Migration Policy Institute: *Fifty Years On, the 1965 Immigration and Nationality Act Continues to Reshape the United States,* Muzaffar Chishti, Faye Hipsman, and Isabel Ball, States, October 15, 2015.

26. Pew Research Center, *America's Dismal Views of the Nation's Politics*, July 2023.

27. Pew Research Center, *Two Decades of Rising Partisan Antipathy*, 2022.

28. R3 Continuum: *Mitigating The Impact of Political and Social Unrest on Employee Mental Health*, April 4, 2004

29. Yukl, G.(1999). An evaluation of conceptual weaknesses in transformational and charismatic leadership theories. *Leadership Quarterly, 10*, 285-305; http://dx.doi.org/10.1016/S1048-9843(99)00013-2

APPENDIX

APPENDIX

CONTENTS **PAGE**

President Donald J. Trump's First 76 Executive Orders

The Office of the Federal Register (OFR) oversees the Federal Register publication system, making available the full text of federal laws and regulations.

As of February 26, 2025, Donald J. Trump has signed 76 Executive orders contained in documents published in the Federal Register. This table contains a listing of all 76 of the signed between January 20, 2025, and February 26, 2025.

Order Record No.	Title	Date Signed
EO 14222	Implementing the President's "Department of Government Efficiency" Cost Efficiency Initiative	February 26, 2025
EO 14221	Making America Healthy Again by Empowering Patients With Clear, Accurate, and Actionable Healthcare Pricing Information	February 25, 2025
EO 14220	Addressing the Threat to National Security From Imports of Copper	February 25, 2025
EO 14219	Ensuring Lawful Governance and Implementing the President's "Department of Government Efficiency" Deregulatory Initiative	February 19, 2025
EO 14218	Ending Taxpayer Subsidization of Open Borders	February 19, 2025
EO 14217	Commencing the Reduction of the Federal Bureaucracy	February 19, 2025
EO 14216	Expanding Access to In Vitro Fertilization	February 18, 2025
EO 14215	Ensuring Accountability for All Agencies	February 18, 2025

Order Record No.	Title	Date Signed
EO 14214	Keeping Education Accessible and Ending COVID-19 Vaccine Mandates in Schools	February 14, 2025
EO 14213	Establishing the National Energy Dominance Council	February 14, 2025
EO 14212	Establishing the President's Make America Healthy Again Commission	February 13, 2025
EO 14211	One Voice for America's Foreign Relations	February 12, 2025
EO 14210	Implementing the President's "Department of Government Efficiency" Workforce Optimization Initiative	February 11, 2025
EO 14209	Pausing Foreign Corrupt Practices Act Enforcement To Further American Economic and National Security	February 10, 2025
EO 14208	Ending Procurement and Forced Use of Paper Straws	February 10, 2025
EO 14207	Eliminating the Federal Executive Institute	February 10, 2025
EO 14206	Protecting Second Amendment Rights	February 7, 2025
EO 14205	Establishment of the White House Faith Office	February 7, 2025
EO 14204	Addressing Egregious Actions of the Republic of South Africa	February 7, 2025
EO 14202	Eradicating Anti-Christian Bias	February 6, 2025
EO 14201	Keeping Men Out of Women's Sports	February 5, 2025
EO 14200	Amendment to Duties Addressing the Synthetic Opioid Supply Chain in the People's Republic of China	February 5, 2025

Order Record No.	Title	Date Signed
EO 14199	Withdrawing the United States From and Ending Funding to Certain United Nations Organizations and Reviewing United States Support to All International Organizations	February 4, 2025
EO 14198	Progress on the Situation at Our Southern Border	February 3, 2025
EO 14197	Progress on the Situation at Our Northern Border	February 3, 2025
EO 14196	A Plan for Establishing a United States Sovereign Wealth Fund	February 3, 2025
EO 14195	Imposing Duties To Address the Synthetic Opioid Supply Chain in the People's Republic of China	February 1, 2025
EO 14194	Imposing Duties To Address the Situation at Our Southern Border	February 1, 2025
EO 14193	Imposing Duties To Address the Flow of Illicit Drugs Across Our Northern Border	February 1, 2025
EO 14192	Unleashing Prosperity Through Deregulation	January 31, 2025
EO 14191	Expanding Educational Freedom and Opportunity for Families	January 29, 2025
EO 14190	Ending Radical Indoctrination in K-12 Schooling	January 29, 2025
EO 14189	Celebrating America's 250th Birthday	January 29,, 2025
EO 14188	Additional Measures To Combat Anti-Semitism	January 29, 2025
EO 14187	Protecting Children From Chemical and Surgical Mutilation	January 28, 2025
EO 14186	The Iron Dome for America	January 27, 2025
EO 14185	Restoring America's Fighting Force	January 27, 2025
EO 14184	Reinstating Service Members Discharged Under the Military's COVID-19 Vaccination Mandate	January 27, 2025
EO 14183	Prioritizing Military Excellence and Readiness	January 27, 2025
EO 14182	Enforcing the Hyde Amendment	January 24, 2025

Order Record No.	Title	Date Signed
EO 14181	Emergency Measures To Provide Water Resources in California and Improve Disaster Response in Certain Areas	January 24, 2025
EO 14180	Council To Assess the Federal Emergency Management Agency	January 24, 2025
EO 14179	Removing Barriers to American Leadership in Artificial Intelligence	January 23, 2025
EO 14178	Strengthening American Leadership in Digital Financial Technology	January 23, 2025
EO 14177	President's Council of Advisors on Science and Technology	January 23, 2025
EO 14176	Declassification of Records Concerning the Assassinations of President John F. Kennedy, Senator Robert F. Kennedy, and the Reverend Dr. Martin Luther King, Jr.	January 23, 2025
EO 14175	Designation of Ansar Allah as a Foreign Terrorist Organization	January 22, 2025
EO 14174	Revocation of Certain Executive Orders	January 21, 2025
EO 14173	Ending Illegal Discrimination and Restoring Merit-Based Opportunity	January 21, 2025
EO 14172	Restoring Names That Honor American Greatness	January 20, 2025
EO 14171	Restoring Accountability to Policy-Influencing Positions Within the Federal Workforce	January 20, 2025
EO 14170	Reforming the Federal Hiring Process and Restoring Merit to Government Service	January 20, 2025
EO 14169	Reevaluating and Realigning United States Foreign Aid	January 20, 2025
EO 14168	Defending Women From Gender Ideology Extremism and Restoring Biological Truth to the Federal Government	January 20, 2025
EO 14167	Clarifying the Military's Role in Protecting the Territorial Integrity of the United States	January 20, 2025
EO 14166	Application of Protecting Americans From Foreign Adversary Controlled Applications Act to TikTok	January 20, 2025

Order Record No.	Title	Date Signed
EO 14165	Securing Our Borders	January 20, 2025
EO 14164	Restoring the Death Penalty and Protecting Public Safety United States Support to All International Organizations	January 20, 2025
EO 14163	Realigning the United States Refugee Admissions Program	January 20, 2025
EO 14162	Putting America First in International Environmental Agreements	January 20, 2025
EO 14161	Protecting the United States From Foreign Terrorists and Other National Security and Public Safety Threats	January 20, 2025
EO 14160	Protecting the Meaning and Value of American Citizenship	January 20, 2025
EO 14159	Protecting the American People Against Invasion	January 20, 2025
EO 14158	Declaring a National Energy Emergency	January 20, 2025
EO 14157	Designating Cartels and Other Organizations as Foreign Terrorist Organizations and Specially Designated Global Terrorists	January 20, 2025
EO 14156	Declaring a National Energy Emergency	January 20, 2025
EO 14155	Withdrawing the United States From the World Health Organization	January 20, 2025
EO 14154	Unleashing American Energy	January 20, 2025
EO 14153	Unleashing Alaska's Extraordinary Resource Potential	January 20, 2025
EO 14152	Holding Former Government Officials Accountable for Election Interference and Improper Disclosure of Sensitive Governmental Information	January 20, 2025

Order Record No.	Title	Date Signed
EO 14151	Ending Radical and Wasteful Government DEI Programs and Preferencing	January 20, 2025
EO 14150	America First Policy Directive to the Secretary of State	January 20, 2025
EO 14149	Restoring Freedom of Speech and Ending Federal Censorship	January 20, 2025

An Early Tracking of President Trump's Executive Actions

As Posted to the Public Domain through a U.S. Congressman's Website as of April 29, 2025.

- **EXECUTIVE ORDERS TARGETING LAW FIRMS**
  Date: March 2025

ACTION: In March 2025, President Donald Trump issued a series of executive orders aimed at prominent law firms, alleging unethical conduct and imposing severe sanctions. These actions included revoking security clearances, terminating government contracts, and restricting access to federal buildings. Notably affected firms include:

Perkins Coie LLP: On March 6, 2025, an executive order barred federal agencies from utilizing Perkins Coie's services, suspended the security clearances of its attorneys, and prohibited its lawyers from entering federal buildings. The administration accused the firm of "dishonest and dangerous activity" and "racial discrimination" related to its diversity initiatives.

Paul, Weiss, Rifkind, Wharton & Garrison: Targeted on March 14, 2025, this firm faced similar retaliatory sanctions due to its pro bono work and associations with individuals involved in investigations against President Trump. The executive order was rescinded after the firm agreed to provide $40 million in pro bono legal services aligned with the administration's agenda and to discontinue its diversity policies.

WilmerHale: On March 27, 2025, an executive order suspended WilmerHale's security clearances, restricted access to federal buildings, and terminated government contracts. The firm was targeted due to its association with former special counsel Robert Mueller, who led the investigation into Russian interference in the 2016 election.

STATUS: These executive orders have sparked significant legal challenges and widespread condemnation from the legal community. Perkins Coie filed a lawsuit resulting in a temporary restraining order blocking most provisions of the executive order against it. Judge Beryl Howell noted that the order *"casts a chilling harm of blizzard proportion across the entire legal profession."* Other firms, such as Jenner & Block, have also initiated legal action, arguing that the administration's actions violate the First Amendment and constitute an abuse of power intended to deter legal opposition.

➢ STRIPPING POWER FROM INDEPENDENT REGULATORY AGENCIES

Date: February 18, 2025

ACTION: President Trump signed an executive order titled, *Ensuring Accountability for All Agencies,* requiring independent regulatory agencies—including the Federal Election Commission (FEC), Federal Communications Commission (FCC), Securities and Exchange Commission (SEC), and Federal Trade Commission (FTC)—to submit their major regulations to the White House Office of Management and Budget (OMB) for review.

The order also mandates that these independent agencies set up new "White House Liaison offices" and coordinate legal positions with the President or Attorney General.

These independent agencies were created by Congress to serve the public interest free from political interference. They are led by experts in their fields and are not meant to be subject to the political whims of any administration. Trump's executive order is widely viewed as an illegal power grab that seeks to erode their independence and bend them to his will.

STATUS: On February 28, 2025, the Democratic National Committee (DNC), along with the Democratic Congressional Campaign Committee (DCCC) and the Democratic Senatorial Campaign Committee (DSCC), filed a lawsuit in the U.S. District Court for the District of Columbia challenging President Trump's Executive Order 14215, titled *"Ensuring Accountability for All Agencies."*

The plaintiffs argue that the order unlawfully extends presidential control over independent agencies, particularly the Federal Election Commission (FEC), thereby undermining their mandated independence.

Legal experts anticipate that the courts will scrutinize the constitutionality of the executive order, especially regarding its impact on the autonomy of independent regulatory agencies. As of March 11, 2025, the case is pending, and no court rulings have been issued yet.

➢ DOGE ACCESS TO GOVERNMENT PAYMENT SYSTEMS

Date: January 31, 2025

ACTION: The Trump Administration granted Elon Musk's Department of Government Efficiency (DOGE) access to sensitive payment and data systems, including those managed by the Treasury Department, Medicare, Medicaid, and Social Security.

STATUS: Congressman Cohen, Rep. Sean Casten (D-IL), and more than 150 House Democrats demanded answers from Treasury Secretary Scott Bessent on Musk's access to government data and payment systems.
On Friday, March 7, a federal judge in Washington, DC refused to block DOGE employees from accessing Treasury payment systems containing Americans' sensitive personal data. However, DOGE's access to the Treasury's payment systems remains blocked under an injunction issued by the Manhattan federal district court in February.

➢ EXECUTIVE ORDER FREEZING FEDERAL GRANT FUNDING

Date: January 27, 2025

ACTION: Trump issued an executive order halting nearly all federal grants, including those funding public health, education, small businesses, and infrastructure projects. This caused deep disruptions across nearly every sector of the economy—temporarily stalling funding for everything from infrastructure projects to lifesaving medical research at St. Jude, UTHSC , and other institutions, and more.

STATUS: On February 3, this was blocked by a federal judge, who ruled that Trump lacked authority to withhold congressionally appropriated funds. While some payments have resumed, delays persist for many programs. Lawsuits were filed by a coalition of 22 state attorneys general, the ACLU, and multiple advocacy groups. Legal challenges remain ongoing.

➢ EXECUTIVE ORDER ENDING BIRTHRIGHT CITIZENSHIP

Date: January 20, 2025

ACTION: Trump issued an executive order attempting to end birthright citizenship for children of non-citizens, a direct violation of the 14th Amendment of the U.S. Constitution.

STATUS: On February 13, 2025, a federal judge, U.S. District Judge Leo Sorokin in Boston, issued a nationwide preliminary injunction blocking President Trump's executive order that sought to end birthright citizenship for children of non-citizens. Judge Sorokin ruled that the order is likely unconstitutional, emphasizing that the 14th Amendment broadly confers birthright citizenship. He is the fourth federal judge to rule against this unconstitutional executive order. As of March 11, 2025, the executive order remains unenforceable due to these injunctions, and legal challenges are ongoing.

➢ CLOSURE OF USAID

Date: February 3, 2025

ACTION: The Trump Administration empowered DOGE to dismantle the U.S. Agency for International Development (USAID), a key institution in foreign aid, including HIV/AIDS prevention programs. The move aimed to significantly reduce the U.S. government's role in international development, halting critical humanitarian aid, disaster relief, and global health initiatives. The decision was met with widespread bipartisan opposition, citing risks to national security and global stability. Many USAID workers are essentially stranded, with no plans from our government to help them travel back to the United States.

STATUS: A federal judge ruled that Trump exceeded his constitutional **authority** by freezing almost all U.S. humanitarian and development spending abroad but did not order the restoration of the terminated contracts. On March 10, 2025, Secretary of State Marco Rubio announced that the Trump administration had completed a six-week purge of USAID programs, eliminating 83% of them and moving the remaining 17% under the State Department. Legal challenges from international aid organizations, advocacy groups, and former USAID officials are ongoing.

FEDERAL WORKERS

➢ THREATENING EMAILS TO FEDERAL WORKERS

Date: January 28, 2025

Action: The Trump Administration sent mass emails encouraging federal workers to resign, with thinly veiled threats of termination. These emails, sent to approximately two million federal employees, warned of impending job cuts and reductions in benefits, creating a climate of fear and uncertainty. Unions and civil service protections groups condemned the move as an intimidation tactic designed to weaken the federal workforce and dismantle career civil service positions.

Status: As of February 12, 2025, approximately 77,000 federal employees — about 3.2% of the workforce — accepted the administration's buyout offer, falling short of the 5-10% target. Legal challenges to the program are ongoing. Legal proceedings remain ongoing.

➢ TERMINATION OF PROBATIONARY EMPLOYEES

DATE: February 13, 2025

Action: The Office of Personnel Management (OPM) and Acting Director Charles Ezell ordered federal agencies to terminate tens of thousands of probationary employees in masse. Probationary employees are members of the competitive service in their first year of employment or of the excepted service in their first two years of employment and may also include long-time federal workers who have recently been employed in a new position or a new agency.

STATUS: On February 28, 2025, a judge ordered that OPM's memos directing the termination of probationary workers were "unlawful, invalid, and must be stopped and rescinded," and that OPM must provide written notice of the order to the six agencies.

PUBLIC HEALTH

➢ ROLLBACK OF HEALTHCARE REGULATIONS

Date: January 25, 2025

ACTION: The Trump Administration issued executive actions rolling back key patient protections under the Affordable Care Act (ACA). These rollbacks eliminate essential health benefits requirements, allowing insurers to once again deny coverage based on pre-existing conditions and impose lifetime coverage limits. The move also defunded ACA outreach programs that help Americans enroll in affordable health plans, threatening access to care for millions.

STATUS: Legal challenges are ongoing. Several state attorneys general, along with healthcare advocacy groups, have filed lawsuits arguing that these actions violate federal law and endanger public health. A preliminary injunction request is under review in multiple courts.
On March 10, 2025, the Trump administration announced further rollbacks, including cuts to ACA enrollment periods and navigator funding. Some states have filed lawsuits to block these changes.

➢ ROLLBACK OF AFFORDABLE DRUG AND INSULIN PRICING POLICIES

Date: January 20, 2025

ACTION: The Trump Administration rescinded Executive Order 14087, which was designed to lower prescription drug costs for Medicare and Medicaid recipients. The rollback eliminated a $2 copayment cap on generic medications for Medicare beneficiaries and terminated a pilot program that helped state Medicaid programs afford expensive but life-saving cell and gene therapies. The order also removed Biden-era policies that allowed Medicare to negotiate lower drug prices for treatments granted accelerated FDA approval.

STATUS: Healthcare advocacy groups and a coalition of state attorneys general have filed lawsuits challenging the rollback, arguing that it unlawfully strips low-income Americans of affordable treatment options. Some states are exploring independent efforts to maintain lower drug costs, but federal support has been withdrawn. Legal challenges remain ongoing.

➢ EXECUTIVE ORDER REMOVING U.S. FROM WHO

Date: January 20, 2025

Action: The Trump Administration announced the withdrawal of the United States from the World Health Organization (WHO), cutting off U.S. funding for global health initiatives, including pandemic preparedness, vaccine distribution, and disease eradication programs. The decision immediately jeopardized global efforts to combat infectious diseases and undermined international health cooperation. Public health experts and bipartisan lawmakers warned that this move could leave the U.S. vulnerable in future health crises.

STATUS: WHO requires a one-year notice before a country can finalize the termination of its membership. Senate Democrats are considering potential legislative action to block the withdrawal and restore funding. Multiple public health organizations and advocacy groups have filed lawsuits challenging the legality of the withdrawal, arguing that it violates congressional mandates on global health commitments.

➢ REDUCING ADMINISTRATIVE SUPPORT FOR NIH GRANTS

Date: February 7, 2025

ACTION: The Trump Administration announced that it will reduce funds that support grants awarded by the National Institutes of Health (NIH) for indirect expenses. Tennessee institutions like St Jude, the University of Tennessee Health Science Center receive $770 million from NIH for medical research grants each year, leading to $1.99 billion in economic activity in our state. The grants include funds for the people conducting the research (direct costs) and also anything that is needed to support the researcher, such as construction, utility costs, safety and security, and the team that supports the researchers (indirect costs). The Trump Administration is limiting indirect expenses to 15% of the grant, a move that would cause layoffs, suspend clinical trials, and delay progress on groundbreaking research.

STATUS: On February 10, Congressman Cohen released a statement stating that the short-sighted and dangerous policy should be reversed immediately. He also signed onto a letter, co-signed by more than 90 of his colleagues in the House of Representatives, to the NIH Acting Director expressing alarm over the decision and requesting information about any downstream impacts NIH considered prior to its announcement. On March 5, 2025, a federal judge in Massachusetts issued a nationwide preliminary injunction blocking the Trump Administration's proposed 15% cap on indirect cost reimbursements for NIH grants. This decision prevents the implementation of the cap, ensuring that for now research institutions will continue to receive necessary funding to support facilities and administrative expenses associated with NIH-funded research.

EDUCATION

➢ EXECUTIVE ORDER TO DISMANTLE THE DEPARTMENT OF EDUCATION

Date: March 20, 2025

ACTION: President Trump signed an executive order directing the closure of the U.S. Department of Education. The order instructs Education Secretary Linda McMahon to take all necessary steps to dismantle the department and "return authority to state and local communities". While the order states that the federal government will maintain essential functions such as Title I funding for low-income schools, Pell Grants, and support for students with disabilities, it will exacerbate educational inequalities and disrupt the administration of vital programs. Concerns have been raised about the future management of the federal student loan portfolio, valued at approximately $1.6 trillion, and the enforcement of civil rights protections in education.

STATUS: The executive order has sparked significant legal and political opposition. A coalition of organizations, including the National Education Association and the NAACP, has filed lawsuits challenging the order, arguing that the dissolution of the Department of Education violates federal statutes and undermines protections for vulnerable student populations. Additionally, since the department was established by Congress, its complete closure would require legislative approval, making the future of this initiative uncertain.

➢ CUTS TO PELL GRANTS AND FEDERAL STUDENT LOAN PROGRAMS

Date: February 5, 2025

Action: The Trump Administration has significantly reduced funding for Pell Grants and other federal student aid programs, making it harder for low-income students to afford higher education. The Department of Education has also introduced new restrictions on federal student loans, capping borrowing limits and tightening eligibility for income-driven repayment plans. These cuts have forced many students to take on more private debt or reconsider their ability to attend college.

Status: Education advocacy groups have filed lawsuits, arguing that these changes violate federal education funding statutes and disproportionately harm low-income students. While some states are exploring ways to supplement lost funding, federal support remains uncertain, leaving current students and families in limbo.

➢ ROLLBACK OF PUBLIC SERVICE LOAN FORGIVENESS AND STUDENT LOAN RELIEF PROGRAMS

Date: February 5, 2025

ACTION: The Trump Administration has moved to dismantle key student loan relief programs, including Public Service Loan Forgiveness (PSLF) and expanded income-driven repayment plans. Borrowers who were on track for forgiveness under PSLF now face uncertainty as the administration seeks to limit eligibility and cancel previously approved relief. Efforts to provide broader student debt cancellation, including relief for borrowers defrauded by for-profit colleges, have also been halted.

STATUS: Multiple lawsuits have been filed by borrowers, advocacy organizations, and state attorneys general, arguing that the rollback violates existing legal protections and disproportionately affects middle- and lower-income Americans. While legal challenges play out, millions of borrowers are left with higher repayment burdens and fewer options for relief.

➢ ATTACKS ON THE DEPARTMENT OF EDUCATION AND LOCKING LAWMAKERS OUT

Date: February 7, 2025

ACTION: The Trump Administration is ramping up its efforts to dismantle the Department of Education, pushing an agenda to gut federal education funding and strip away student protections. Reports indicate the administration is preparing an executive order to shut down the department entirely, handing control over to states—many of which have already slashed public school budgets and rolled back civil rights protections.
Adding to the chaos, **congressional** lawmakers were locked out of the Department of Education when they attempted to meet with agency officials to demand answers. Trump's team is not only gutting critical student aid programs but actively blocking elected representatives from doing their jobs and holding them accountable.

STATUS: The administration's radical push to eliminate the Department of Education has drawn fierce backlash. Legal experts have pointed out that **abolishing a federal agency requires congressional approval**, making this another reckless political stunt. Meanwhile, shutting lawmakers out of a federal agency is unprecedented and raises serious questions about transparency and accountability. House Democrats are calling for immediate oversight hearings and demanding the administration reverse course before millions of students and borrowers suffer the consequences. The fight to protect public education is far from over—but make no mistake, Trump and his allies want to tear it down brick by brick.

ENVIRONMENTAL PROTECTIONS

➢ ROLLBACK OF EPA REGULATIONS

Date: February 4, 2025

ACTION: The Trump Administration issued sweeping rollbacks to environmental protections, weakening regulations on air and water quality, allowing increased industrial pollution, and reversing emissions standards for power plants and vehicles. The Environmental Protection Agency (EPA) was ordered to halt enforcement of climate-related policies, and several clean energy funding programs were defunded. These changes sparked widespread concern among environmental organizations, health experts, and state governments.

STATUS: Executive order in effect. Lawsuits have been filed by multiple states, environmental advocacy groups, and public health organizations. A federal court has scheduled hearings on an emergency injunction request, but the policy changes remain in effect for now. Legal challenges remain ongoing.

➢ WITHDRAWAL FROM PARIS CLIMATE ACCORDS

Date: January 22, 2025

ACTION: The Trump Administration formally withdrew the United States from the Paris Climate Agreement, reversing years of progress on global climate commitments.

STATUS: The executive order remains in effect. Senate Democrats are pushing legislative measures to rejoin the agreement, while multiple states and environmental groups have filed lawsuits challenging the legality of the withdrawal. Several states, including California and New York, have announced independent commitments to meet Paris Agreement goals despite the federal withdrawal.

➢ CUTS TO CLEAN ENERGY AND SUSTAINABILITY PROGRAMS

Date: February 2, 2025

Action: The Trump Administration slashed funding for federal clean energy and sustainability programs, including initiatives aimed at expanding renewable energy infrastructure, improving energy efficiency, and reducing carbon emissions. Programs supporting wind and solar development, climate resilience projects, and electric vehicle infrastructure were among those defunded, putting thousands of clean energy jobs at risk.

Status: Lawsuits challenging the budget cuts have been filed by multiple states, clean energy organizations, and environmental advocacy groups, arguing that these reductions violate federal mandates on climate policy. A federal court has yet to rule on an emergency injunction request.

SMALL BUSINESSES

- **Cuts to Small Business Grants, Including Black- and Women-Owned Businesses**

Date: February 1, 2025

ACTION: The Trump Administration halted funding for federal small business grants, disproportionately impacting minority- and women-owned businesses that rely on these programs for startup capital, expansion, and stability. The cuts have particularly targeted initiatives aimed at fostering economic growth in historically underserved communities. The administration has also moved to eliminate funding tied to diversity, equity, and inclusion (DEI) programs.

STATUS: As of March 11, 2025, the Trump Administration's funding freeze on federal small business grants, including those supporting minority- and women-owned businesses, remains blocked by federal court orders. Multiple lawsuits have been filed by higher education and civil rights advocacy groups, arguing that the cuts violate federal economic equity mandates.

TRANSFORMATIONAL LEADERSHIP COMPARED TO OTHER STYLES

Transformational Leadership	The Leader creates substantial change for team members as well as organizations and motivates and inspires them to reach extraordinary success. Expectations, aspirations, perceptions, and values are transformed into something better.
Democratic Leadership	The Leader builds on empowering team members to participate in decision-making, with a strive toward consensus.
Affiliative Leadership	The Leader is completely focused on the people and relationships in an organization.
Coaching Leadership	The Leader focuses on improving employees to become better individuals and professionals with the leader as a coach.
Visionary Leadership	The Leader focuses on the long-term results and builds on participation, communication, and goal setting.
Commanding Leadership	The Leader maintains tight control with high clarity in rules, roles, and expectations and makes all the decisions.
Servant Leadership	The Leader focuses on improving people, society, and organizations and serves others, which leads to strong ethics, and engaged, motivated employees.
Pacesetting Leadership	The Leader sets an example of high performance, pace, and quality.
Transactional Leadership	The Leader builds a clear structures of rewards and punishment for different levels of performance and focuses on results, efficiency, and performance rather than people and relationships.
Laissez-Faire Leadership	The Leader is "hands-off" and gives team members the freedom to make all decisions. Laissez-faire leadership can work with highly skilled, capable, and self-motivated individuals and teams.
Autocratic Leadership	The Leader holds all the decision power, rarely consults others, which leads to low engagement and sometimes create toxic environments. This style is useful in a crisis when control and fast decisions are crucial.

Task-Oriented Leadership	The Leader is all about getting the job done, task execution, quality, output, and other non-human aspects, while putting a lower priority on relationships and people.
Relationship-Oriented Leadership	The Leader has a strong focus on developing bonds and relationships with team members and other stakeholders, which leads to trust, friendship, and a supporting team climate.
Telling/Directive Leadership	The Leader tells team members what to do and when to do it in a "guiding way." The focus on the team members can actively learn from the leader.
Bureaucratic Leadership	The Leader favors rigid rules, high standardization, and stiff division of labor, which often hampers change, creativity, competition, and development.

www.ingramcontent.com/pod-product-compliance
Lightning Source LLC
LaVergne TN
LVHW090608110826
845146LV00001B/308

9798992899603